ARE YOU THE NEXT CEO?

A Guide to **Starting** a **Business** and **Becoming** a **Successful Entrepreneur**

PRASHANTHI KOLLURU

INDIA • SINGAPORE • MALAYSIA

Notion Press

No. 8, 3rd Cross Street
CIT Colony, Mylapore
Chennai, Tamil Nadu – 600004

First Published by Notion Press 2021
Copyright © Prashanthi Kolluru 2021
All Rights Reserved.

ISBN 978-1-63745-478-7

This book has been published with all efforts taken to make the material error-free after the consent of the author. However, the author and the publisher do not assume and hereby disclaim any liability to any party for any loss, damage, or disruption caused by errors or omissions, whether such errors or omissions result from negligence, accident, or any other cause.

While every effort has been made to avoid any mistake or omission, this publication is being sold on the condition and understanding that neither the author nor the publishers or printers would be liable in any manner to any person by reason of any mistake or omission in this publication or for any action taken or omitted to be taken or advice rendered or accepted on the basis of this work. For any defect in printing or binding the publishers will be liable only to replace the defective copy by another copy of this work then available.

CONTENTS

Acknowledgments.......................................7
Introduction 9

1. **A Few Slips When Starting Up a Business** 11
   Idea of Continuous Pursuit......................11
   Need for Systems and Process and Finances 14
   Keep Yourself Updated 16
   It is Quite Interesting, Isn't It?....................26
   My Startup Story 26
   Key Takeaways 30

2. **The Essentials of Business**......................31
   What to Start With? How to Start a Business?.......31
   Choosing the Right Partner......................39
   How to Identify the Right Partner? 39
   Key Takeaways 40

3. **Marketing "The Ignored Pillar"** 41
   A Big Differentiator Between Success and Survival ...41
   Marketing......................................41
   Key Takeaways 50

4. **Sales – Treasure Chest of Your Business** 51
   Sales 51
   What Are Marketing Leads? 52

    What Are Sales Leads?........................53
    FAQs 57
    Common Mistakes Done 59
    Why Should You Qualify or Disqualify a Prospect?...64
    Handling Objections 64

5. **Customer Service**............................67
    The Overlooked Chapter in Business 67
    Customer Service 67
    How to Start with Customer Service? 69

6. **Leadership**..................................71
    The Essential Pillar of the Business................71
    Leadership 71

7. **Finance and Cash-Flows** 79
    The Un-Compromised Pillar 79
    Getting Your Numbers Right 82
    Is Bootstrapping a Good Idea for Your Business?.....83
    What is Bootstrapping?.........................83

8. **Stages of Business from Startup to Sustainable** 85

9. **What Should You Do When You Are Stuck?**........93

10. **Finding Your Why?** 97
    Clarity of Thought 101
    Attitude to Learn and Share 101
    Toughness to Endure and Thrive.................102
    Networking as a Leader in Business...............102
    Storytelling as An Art of Leadership 103
    Why is Storytelling Important?..................103
    Why Context?................................104
    Content 105

Conclusion 105
Passion and Purpose 106
Purpose. 108
Discipline 109

11. Risk Tolerance for Entrepreneurs 111

12. Identifying Your Strengths .117

13. Mindset vs. Skill-Set 121

14. Power of Leverage 127
What Were the Leverages That Gates Had?. 130

15. Importance of a Mentor 133
Why Does a Business Owner Need a Mentor? 134

16. Why Perfectionists May Find It Difficult to Thrive in Business? 137
What is Success in Life or Business? 138

Final Words. 141
Short Poem Dedicated to Entrepreneurs. 143
About the Author. 145

ACKNOWLEDGMENTS

Any work is impossible without a team. This book is no exception. I would like to thank my family, friends, colleagues and associates who have contributed in their own way in making this book come to life.

I owe an enormous debt of gratitude to those who gave me detailed and constructive comments on one or more chapters, including Ms. Priyamvada Bulusu, Ms. Padma Akula, and Vijaya Reddy. I would like to thank Ms. Vidya Vellala, Founder of FaastHelp, for giving me insights into her experience in her journey of entrepreneurship and allowing me to present her viewpoints in this book. I got an opportunity to discuss the nuances of the text and to clarify concepts. I would also like to thank all those people who motivated me to stand for myself. I would like to acknowledge the hard work put in by my editorial team lead by Ms. Juhi Dhruva, Mr. Vivek Menon and Ms. Saheefa from Notion Press Team.

Finally, I want to thank my dear husband, Srini, for tolerating my incessant disappearances into my home office. A lifelong partner makes my journey worth discovering at every step. My heartfelt gratitude to my mom, my dad and my son Chandra Siddharth, who constantly supported me in my journey thus far.

INTRODUCTION

Many of us are passionate to solve problems. Whatever background we come from, when we see a problem, we subconsciously also think of solutions. The same thing happened to me. I saw a problem. I found a solution. I built that solution but failed. The failure was not in the solution, but in taking it to the market.

When this happened, I did not know what to do. I was trying to take it to the market, by talking to different people, showcasing my demo and convincing them that there is a solution that I can help with. I realized I was talking to the wrong people. My approach was wrong and there was something that was lacking.

When I looked around and talked to entrepreneurs, I understood, I was not alone. This is what many passionate entrepreneurs face. We give our 100% in building the solutions, and then when it comes to selling the solution, we fail.

That is when I realized that Marketing and Sales are the two biggest pillars of any business. My passion is to educate fellow entrepreneurs to enable them to keep enough resources for Marketing and Sales. Today I work with many businesses helping them market their SaaS, E-commerce products and taking them to the market.

Businesses start and fail. I was on the verge of failure too. But I stood up, brushed up myself, and I am back on track. Many startup enthusiasts see only the cream that is visible on the top. They do not realize that there is a lot of hard work, a teamwork, leverage, patience and perseverance that goes in.

My intention in writing this book is to help startup enthusiasts with the basics of business. What is that you need to start with, what are the personality traits you need to have and how you should go about it.

In this book, I help you understand the journey of many entrepreneurs, who were on the path of success, those who failed and quit and those who failed and then chose to succeed. You will see many stories, which may resonate with you, your feelings, situations and emotions.

So let's begin this book, to learn more and understand what business is all about.

Chapter 1
A FEW SLIPS WHEN STARTING UP A BUSINESS

Idea of Continuous Pursuit

It was mid-summer. Sasha and John were seeing each other for quite some time. Sasha had just come back from work. Sasha was a user experience designer working at a banking company. John lost his job during the 2008 recession. He could not find anything soon. John was working as a data analyst for a market research company when he lost his job. He had close to seven years' experience.

His friends Ron and Nick were working elsewhere. Every time the three of them met, they vaguely discussed starting up their own business. Their discussions mostly revolved around startups, funding, investments, etc. While Ron and Nick were only considering it as an idea, John had already started to conceptualize the idea. He was working on starting up on his own.

It was mid-October, 2008. John called upon Ron and Nick for a meeting at a coffee shop. They planned to meet at 11 A.M. at Starbucks that just opened a week ago in San Palo suburbs. Ron and Nick arrived and saw John was waiting anxiously, with few papers in hand. They understood that John wanted to discuss something really important. They quickly ordered some coffee and started the discussion.

John said, "Guys, we have always been discussing starting up our own business. While we were discussing, I was already working on a few things. I would like to discuss with you guys today. Please give me your honest feedback."

Ron said, "Okay, John, that's great. Please let us know what help you need."

John pulled out his papers and showed them his plan of starting up a kid's store which would sell toys and kids stationery. He told them about his plan of scaling up, opening multiple stores in multiple locations, etc. They discussed in detail, most of the business aspects including procurement, supply chain logistics, etc. It was a three-hours'-discussion, and finally, Ron and Nick were convinced that John had indeed worked hard to put up the plan.

Nick said, "Well, John, you have indeed worked really hard to put all this together. Appreciate it, man!"

Ron asked, "How do you want to get started? Do you have any investors who can fund you for the project?"

John said, "Yes, I am looking for help from you guys!. Would you be able to fund this project? I am really looking forward to working with you guys."

Ron and Nick just had their "Stop Moment".

Nick said, "Come on John, we were indeed discussing all the interesting things during our previous conversations. But we never intended to invest our hard-earned money"

Ron added, "Moreover John, we do not even know if this idea will work. How can we invest and risk ourselves?"

They both advised John to find his own investors.

John was taken by surprise. He said to himself "Oh My God, what was I thinking? I just gave in to their idea of starting up, without understanding their intention."

John apologized for having ambushed them without giving them a context of the meeting.

He felt embarrassed. He left the meeting with a feeling of pain and guilt. He had believed that his friends would be interested in starting up and would help him set up things. This meeting cleared the air. He understood that they never intended to start/invest in a business at all.

John discussed with Sasha about what had happened. She was quite supportive and asked "So, what's your plan? Do you really want to start your own business?"

John was not sure. He replied "Let me think about it and let you know"

Sasha was prepared to take a "Yes" or "No". She was ready to find the required funding to help John. However, John felt he was not ready. He continued his search for a job.

Two weeks later, he received a call for an interview. He did it well and got hired at another market research company.

Today he works as a data scientist at a reputed market research firm that works on building AI/ML products. Surrounded by good colleagues, John feels happy with his career. He meets Ron and Nick over the weekends.

He never pursued that dream of starting up on his own again.

Mistake #1: Giving up too early.

It is not only John, we all give up on our dreams too quickly. We attribute our failure to pursue our dreams to external sources like friends, family, markets, government, etc. However, we never accept that we did not have enough strength to pursue it further. Do you relate yourself to the story of John?

Never give up on your dreams!

Check out the story of Anitha, who started her business, but failed. What made her fail, even after she pursued her dream?

* * *

Need for Systems and Process and Finances

Anita was working at a kids' playschool. She was working there for the past ten years. She knew the in-and-out of running a playschool.

During her vacation with a few of her friends, she discussed her idea of starting up her own school. All her friends supported her. She went ahead, raised some funds through her local church and community. She got started.

She rented a beautiful property in the midst of the suburbs. She worked hard to finalize on the concepts like a brand for her school. Her community and her church gave her enough support and ecosystem. She invited a Senator to open the facility. Many of her friends and family turned up for the event. She was so happy to see everyone around. She thanked each and every one for coming in support of her.

Anita hired a good number of teachers. She had a few children already enrolled from the next day. She knew in her mind that she had enough cash-flows for the next six months' time. She set up a goal of breaking even before six months and getting into the profit mode.

She planned everything cautiously. However, her limited financial sources did not give her the liberty to spend enough on Marketing activities. A couple of bad reviews on the school turned down the prospects. She was unable to breakeven after six months. Her overhead costs were biting back. She struggled with cash-flows. By ten months, the next summer, she gave up on her business.

She realized that she had to set up a proper system in place to run a school. A dream of running a school was not just enough. She had to build a few skills, acquire knowledge to run it successfully. It was too overwhelming for her to work on a few areas that she never worked on. She had difficulty in delegating the financial aspects, Marketing, managing online reputation, etc.

The power of pursuit has an important role to play in the life of an entrepreneur. That is human nature. Unfortunately, we all forget that we fell several times before we started walking on our own. We practiced standing up several times when we were children. For some of us, it took weeks to put our first foot forward and then the next and then the next. We fell at every step, but we learned how to walk. We learn and unlearn a few things, we fall, we fail but there is always a choice. You can raise and take the next step, or accept yourself and stay where you are. The same is with the journey of entrepreneurship. Some fail early, learn and move forward, while some accept and move on.

Coming to learning, it is a flow. The moment we stop learning, we find there is suffocation ahead. Usually, many of us stop learning after we have left our college. We enter life, thinking we know everything. But life is a bigger teacher. It shows your mistakes differently and makes sure you realize them by yourself. Here is the story of Sarit, his realization of being stuck and what he learned in his career and life?

* * *

Keep Yourself Updated
Sarit started working with one of the healthcare companies in the US, right after college. He was a bright student and had all the qualities of an entrepreneur. He was self-motivated, self-disciplined and dedicated to his work. He always had a dream of starting up his own company.

As days passed by, Sarit got married and started his family. After eight years of successfully serving his company, he moved up the ladder and was the lead architect for IT services. He mostly worked on COBOL and Mainframe systems. Newer technologies or platforms never attracted his attention. He felt comfortable with his existing role. As days passed by, he felt his job was no longer satisfying. Though he spent most of the day guiding his team, he felt hollow. His work was not exciting him anymore.

It was a weekend. Sarit and his wife planned for a trip to Chicago to visit their old friends Amit and Madhur. They reached Chicago on a Friday evening. All his friends were mostly his ex-colleagues. They had left their jobs at the healthcare company and moved on for better opportunities.

The next morning, as the wives prepared breakfast, chatting in the kitchen, the guys were sitting in the porch enjoying the view of downtown Chicago.

Amit, Madhur and Sarit were discussing their work, cracking a few jokes about their teams and workplaces. It was a casual conversation. Sarit was actively participating in the discussion. Slowly the conversation turned toward experience and the old technologies that are getting outdated.

Sarit felt uncomfortable when he heard about the technologies getting outdated. He subconsciously began to worry. He had a feeling that something was not right with his career. He stopped talking and fell into deep thought. He started asking himself, "Am I enjoying my work at this company? Why don't I feel excited about my work anymore? What is stopping me from exploring other opportunities?". Though he was physically present listening to his friends, his mind was wandering looking for answers.

He was waiting to get back to his home, where he could get quite some time to think.

It was already Sunday. Sarit and his wife initially planned to start post-lunch. However, these questions kept Sarit restless for the whole time and he wanted to start a little earlier.

As he was driving home, these questions came back again and again. Sarit's wife understood that something was bothering him. However, she did not want to disturb him after he did not answer a couple of her questions.

Sarit sat down with a pen and paper. He wrote down all the things that kept him excited during his initial days at work. How he was excited to learn, how he wanted to solve problems quickly and how he would find optimized solutions that kept the technology workflows small, easy and efficient.

As he was writing, he slowly realized that the job was making him too comfortable. There were lesser and lesser problems to solve every day. Most of the work he was doing, was just managing people. His enthusiasm to solve problems was not found in his work equation. Since he knew all the systems and their challenges end-to-end, his work became too comfortable. Little did he realize that he had become too comfortable with his current job. He never thought of quitting or changing his job.

As this dawned upon him, Sarit started to feel bored doing the same work. His conscious mind was not in sync with the subconscious. He started to fail in delivering up to his manager's expectations. Soon he realized, it was time for him to take the leap.

Sarit started applying for opportunities at other companies. Every time he attended an interview call, he felt restless. He realized that his experience was not sufficient to get a new opportunity. The market demanded more than just the experience he carried. There had been many advancements in technology. Most of the companies were moving away from COBOL and adopting new technologies. The opportunities for a COBOL Architect were less-found.

Sarit realized that he made a big mistake by not keeping himself aware of the market happenings. He decided something must change. He started listing down his experiences at his interviews and analyzed what the market was looking for. He started focusing all his time and energy on learning new technologies. He realized that many companies were looking to either get away with COBOL or build hybrid solutions that work along with COBOL. Sarit designed architectural solutions around these use-cases. He started talking about his passion for solving this market problem. He landed up with an opportunity at First US Bank.

He realized the importance of learning and keeping himself updated about the latest happenings in his area of expertise.

Today he blocks his calendar for two hours every week, to keep himself abreast of happenings in his area of expertise. He attends many online sessions and seminars to keep himself updated. With his acquired knowledge, he established his expertise. Today he is invited to give guest lectures at technology events. He has been successfully consulting for many startups, medium and large enterprises. Though his dream of becoming an entrepreneur never came true, he is happy to serve the entrepreneurial community with his knowledge and expertise. He helps startups with designing software architecture. His consultation work for large enterprises includes technology optimization, functional and system optimization.

As you saw, John, Anita and Sarit had their own challenges in getting started and living their dreams. We come across these situations and circumstances in our lives too.

We all aspire to become successful. But then why do we fail? What is the difference between those who get started and those who don't? What is it that successful people carry and people who fail don't? What is the difference?

Sherin's circumstances were no different from many of us. But let's see what she has done when it came to her life and business.

* * *

As days passed by, she thought how wonderful her life has turned out to be. She was wondering, "What would have happened if I never started? Where would I be, if I had not started this business?" She was so happy for the team of women who were just walking into the office, taking their seats to begin their day's work.

Sherin started her business ten years ago when she was just dreaming to start one. She did not have a perfect plan, but she knew she had to start somewhere. She had been planning something for a few years by then.

Sherin came from a small town, where girls were allowed to complete their tenth grade. Studying beyond tenth grade was a difficult task. However, Sherin's parents were educated. They understood that the only property they could pass on to their children was giving them a proper education and let them explore their dreams and passions.

Sherin always felt fortunate about being born in such a family. She always felt grateful toward her parents, teachers and friends who always kept her motivated.

With unwavering support from her parents, Sherin chased her dreams. She did her post-graduation from a prestigious University. During her higher studies, she was known very well among all her mates. She was active in studies and co-curricular activities. Having won many competitions, she was well-known to her teachers and professors as well.

However, everything changed in May 2004, when she had one question in front of her—"What next after post-graduation? What should I do?" She had no clue. She had many options to go about—become a professor, get into banking, or get married, as most of her classmates chose.

But she ruled out all the options and chose to appear for the Indian Civil Service exam. She felt she had the responsibility to give back to her country and people. Getting into Civil Service would give her an opportunity to do greater good and reach as many people as possible. She made a sincere attempt at the exam. But destiny had a different plan for her.

She started working in an MNC. She made really good friends. There were married people, there were bachelors, there were different people with different ideas. Finally, in 2008 October, she got married to the wonderful person of her dreams—Harshad.

Harshad was already working for an MNC by then. He had met Sherin a couple of times before her proposed to her for marriage. They got married in 2008 October with families from both sides accepting their wishes.

Sherin was good at writing English, communicating well in the English language and was comfortable in copy-writing and editing. When Harshad was deputed to the US on a work assignment, Sherin accompanied him along with their son Anish who was just seven months old.

Sherin had a passion to contribute something to the greater good. She felt everyone has a purpose and that every day is a blessing. She wanted to make the best utilization of her skills and knowledge. She did not want to just sit at home and do nothing. She was passionate, wanted to be independent. That did not mean she wanted to do everything on her own. She always looked for support from her husband, who never said "no" to her.

It was September 2010: Sherin was anxiously waiting for Harshad to return from his office. It was a Friday, and Harshad would come back usually by 4:30 P.M. They had a weekend trip planned to Sedona, AZ along with a group of friends. Sherin had already packed everything, and they were planning to start by 6 P.M. Sedona is a two-hour' drive from Phoenix. Sherin was so looking forward to the trip.

It was around 4:25 P.M. that Harshad returned from his office. He was also excited about the trip, as he was looking forward to spending time with his best buddies.

As planned they started at 6 P.M. As they crossed the city and were on the Highway, Sherin thought that was the best time to tell Harshad. Sherin was excited and scared to share her thoughts. She knew deep in her heart that Harshad would not say no. She was hopeful.

She started with a casual conversation. She asked, "Harshad, how was your office today?"

Harshad replied, "It was a busy day. We had a few releases that were planned last week. They troubled us a little. The whole week, we tried fixing them. I am so glad to have this stress-relieving trip"

Sherin was a little doubtful if that was a good time. But as always, she said, "Harshad, I want to tell you something. But promise me, you will not scold or get upset about it."

Harshad said, "OK".

Every time Sherin said that Harshad was already prepared in his mind not to disappoint Sherin.

Sherin said, "Harshad, I wanted to start my own copy-writing business. I would like to know your thoughts about it."

Sherin kept her fingers crossed, and was waiting for him to reply. She was nervous, excited and eager.

Harshad said "Okay, great! That's quite surprising. So how do you want to start?"

Sherin felt happy that Harshad was positive about her idea. They started discussing at length about how she should start, what she should look for and how to go about it.

Sherin had already collected all the information about how to start a company in the US. She registered herself as a C-Corp and got in touch with a few of her friends who were willing to start working with her immediately. She got her website designed, started with a minimum budget and marketed her services online. "Finding my first client was my business breakthrough," she recollects. It took them three-four months to find their first client. And Sherin's team knew it was just the beginning. And true to their beliefs, there was no looking back from then.

Today, Sherin runs an agency with top content writers, copywriters and digital Marketing experts. She takes pride in her all-women team and finds it really easy to collaborate.

As you must have observed, John, Sarit and Anita were having a problem with starting up a business.

While John was passionate, he did not reach out to the right people. And he never tried enough to pursue his dreams. He gave up too early in the game.

Sarit was stuck in his comfort zone for a long time. His risk appetite was already down. However, he started learning after having realized his mistakes.

Anita on the other hand started the business just because she had expertise in the area of administration. But she could not pursue further, as she did not plan beyond eighteen months.

While John, Sarit and Anita made a few starting-up mistakes, Sherin planned things carefully.

Many startups get killed in the idea-stage itself. Here is why:

- Discuss the idea with the wrong people.
- Do research online and find that an idea failed.
- Do enough research and ascertain that this might not work.
- After a few days, the fire inside dies, so does the idea.
- Sometimes, we overcome all the above and start working on the idea, but get distracted, or lose the will to pursue it further.

As Mr. Narayana Murthy, Chairman Emeritus recently quoted, entrepreneurship is all about thinking the other way round. It is about asking yourself "Why my idea won't succeed? How should I make it work". That is how Sherin did. She found every possible way to continue her passion. Her passion to contribute to the greater good always kept her motivated.

Here are a few statistics about startups for your reference.

- Only 10% of the new startups succeed.
- **25% of venture-backed startups** succeed.
- Under **50% of businesses** make it to their fifth year.
- **33% of startups** make it to the ten-year mark.
- Only **40% of startups** actually turn a profit.
- **82% of businesses** that fail do so because of cash-flow problems.
- The highest failure rate occurs in the Information industry (**63%**).

[Source review42.com and medium.com]

We all must have read these statistics at some point in our life. And most of us usually look at the 90% of the startups that failed. We are scared if we might fall into the failed category. But the truth is, they did not pursue enough to fall into the 10% success category.

Here are a few circumstantial or emotional reasons why many people want to start their business:

- Emotional or Impulsive Start. Give in to emotions saying "Mr. X started with his business. He earns a lot of money. I also want to start and earn a lot of money."
- Starting up with an intent to prove something. Attitude to prove that they can also start their business and prove to the world.

- Starting up to just tell the world that he/she is into business. Give an identity to self.
- Have a business idea and a plan. Really have an idea and want to solve a problem. Do whatever it takes to solve a problem.

It is Quite Interesting, Isn't It?

When starting up a business it is always a spring, with beautiful ideas. New people coming into your life, you start with your product or service and try finding your customers. My startup was no different.

However, the first roadblock most businesses see is in the first six months. Here could be the reason for the roadblock you may see:

- Financial roadblock
- People roadblock
- Product roadblock

My Startup Story

It was in February 2009. My husband and I were taking a stroll in the nearby park when my husband said, "What do you think, if I quit my job and start my own company?". We were just a few months into our marriage. We had not even set up our home. I said "I think it's too early for you to start your own company." There were several 'what if's' in our conversation that day. We had a long discussion around what would we need for the next five years, how we would plan our family, etc., However, we agreed on one point. One of us would work if the other would take up business.

In 2009 December, we registered our first company. Took up a few software projects and delivered to the clients. We partnered with one of our friends, who agreed to work for the company full-time, while we would support the company.

He worked hard to get the projects and deliver them. We hired a few engineers who had passed out of college and were passionate to learn and excel.

It was in October 2012, when he called quits. We tried to understand and solve things for him. But he was no longer driven by the passion to continue. We closed the company in 2012. Then we were again back to square one. People and Financial roadblock.

By then we were working in the US, we were bound by our visas. Hence we decided to move back to India in 2013. But the fire to own our business was still there. Having learned a few lessons from our first failure, we found a few gaps in ourselves and our skillsets.

Here were the few gaps we found:
- Marketing Strategy
- Sales Pipeline
- Right People
- Cash-Flows

Our strong areas were technology and delivery. But we were weak in the above areas.

We had two choices to fill those gaps:
1. Go to a college, get an MBA and restart
2. Join a startup, and learn on the field.

We chose the second one.

I worked in a couple of startups. I realized that there were several things to learn, there was no hard and fast rule that business should be run in a particular way. I devoted my time to learn and fill those gaps.

Finally in May 2014, we started our second company KloudPortal.

We just started with bootstrapping and building our own SaaS product. We developed a product called FALCON. This product was for stock market tips providers.

We went ahead with the entire product development. Hired a team of software engineers and got the software developed. We spent our savings on building the product. We successfully launched the product with a good PR strategy. But unfortunately, we failed once again

Six months after the product launch, we were unable to sell even a single license. We did not know where to find our customers. Here is what we realized:

- Product-Market fit analysis was not done. We were too early into the market. The market was not looking for this product.
- We outsourced Sales, making sure we do not do the same mistake as earlier. But unfortunately, we never knew how to measure the Sales team's performance.
- We designed the Marketing strategy, but unfortunately, Marketing strategy was incorrect. It did not have the follow-up plans. "What if this strategy failed?" we never asked this question to ourselves.
- Not enough cash-flows to take the product into the market.

If you are already running a startup, I am sure, you will relate to the mistakes we had committed. It is not you alone, there are many people who probably commit similar mistakes and sometimes give up mid-way.

Coming back to the top mistakes and our realizations, the TOP few mistakes we committed again were:

- Did not know how to measure Sales activities and track their performance.
- Market analysis was missing yet again.
- Did not plan for Marketing and Sales expenses.
- Not enough cash-flows to take the product to market.

What did we learn?

- Developing a software product needs continuous cash-flows. It is not a one-time done-and-dusted job.
- Sales and Marketing budgets are never to be ignored.
- Hiring the right people for the right job is important.
- Have a proper Marketing plan along with strategy. Always be ready to tweak your strategy, to get the desired output. Sometimes, you may have to experiment with smaller budgets.

And those were the roadblocks we faced in six-twelve months and unfortunately, we gave up…!

We gave up the product, but not the dream.

Our drive to build products to solve a common man's problems was never-ending. We started building another product for schools, teachers and educational institutions. We started adding more and more SaaS products to our digital catalog. Apart from Marketing on our own, we also tied up with a marketplace where people could find our products.

The happiest moment was when we saw our first sale in the marketplace. People started buying, asking for customizations for our products.

You may ask me "How did you manage the cash-flows when you were developing those SaaS products after all those failures?"

Well, you are right. That is when we realized the importance of having a services team along with a product team. This has helped us counter-balance most of our cash-flows.

Today I work with a passion and a vision. My mission is very simple—"EVERY STARTUP SHOULD SURVIVE AND THRIVE". We help startups to build, market and service their products. The dream inside every business owner is to solve a problem in the market. But unfortunately, not many products see the light due to various reasons. Our mission is to help startups get their product into the market.

Key Takeaways

1. If you have a passion to start your business, then just START. Take that First Step.
2. Learn from your mistakes.
3. Plan for eighteen months.
4. Focus on your plan.
5. Have Marketing and Sales budgets planned.
6. Have the right team in place.
7. If you are a product company, ensure you have enough cash-flows to survive and breakeven.
8. Trust your instincts and get ahead in the game!

* * *

Chapter 2

THE ESSENTIALS OF BUSINESS

What to Start With? How to Start a Business?

Robert was in his mid-thirties. He was a Sales head working with one of the high-end cars company in Detroit. He started right after college and had close to eight years' experience in Sales. His managers loved him a lot, as he was one of their top performers. He had an art of selling a high-end car in the showroom to the toughest customer. And this he used to do with ease!

Robert's wife Laura was a kindergarten teacher. She loved spending time with the children. They were a happy couple enjoying their working lives and vacation days.

As days passed, they decided to start their family. They welcomed their daughter Tiara into their life. It was almost twelve years by then. Robert was still working in that same car company. Though he enjoyed his job, lately he started feeling something was not right. Laura had left her job to take care of Tiara, and Robert could not convince his boss on a pay rise and commission. It was tough for Robert to handle the expenses with a nanny, a day-job, the home loan, etc. Though Robert had enough savings by then, he was not sure where he was heading to.

Robert wanted to discuss his situation with one of his old friends Bill. Bill lived in San Francisco and was traveling to Detroit on a business trip. Bill had his own business by then. Though Bill was not running into profits, he was fairly breaking even to run it for a longer time.

Having known that Bill would be in the town the following week, Robert invited Bill to his home for dinner. Laura had met Bill on their wedding day and had not seen him after that. Robert felt it would be a good reunion too.

Bill agreed to visit Robert, but on one condition. Bill wanted to have his favorite dish prepared by Robert, as he did during his dorm days! Robert agreed.

Bill had already made all his plans for the trip and reserved one day to spend with Robert and Laura. He completed all his appointments and on the last day of the trip visited Robert and Laura. The hosts were very happy to see Bill after a long time. They had a casual talk about parents, siblings, friends and other memories while having their dinner.

As Laura and Tiara headed to bed, Robert sat with Bill to discuss what was bothering him. He explained to him about everything that was going on in his life and work. Bill reprimanded Robert for sticking to the same company for a long time. He said, "When you stick with the same company, neither the company grows nor do you grow after a certain time". For Robert, it was an eye-opener. He never thought about it that way.

Robert asked, "Bill, I would like to start my own company, do you think it is a good time to start?" Bill replied, "Robert, there is never a good time or bad time to start on your own.

The only thing you should know is what you want to start with, and do you have enough funds to survive till your business breaks even?"

Robert was quite surprised. He said, "Why do I need to have enough finances to start on my own? I can borrow some funds from my friends and get started."

Bill quickly asked "So what is your business all about? What is that you want to start and who are your target customers?"

Robert was excited, as Bill was curious to know more "Bill, I have been into Sales for a large part of my life. I feel there is a huge gap in training Salespeople. I can teach a bunch of guys, on how to sell."

Bill replied "That's fantastic. But who are your audience? Whom are you going to teach?"

Robert already expected this question from Bill. He was waiting to answer "Bill, immediate college pass-outs are my ideal clients. I can train them to become the best Salespeople."

Bill understood that Robert needs to do more homework.

Bill asked a few more questions, like who would be his paying customers, how he would scale up his business, and why he was so passionate to start this business. All these questions made Robert think and drove him to do his homework.

Having spoken to Bill, he understood that there was a lot of work he had to do before he started up on his own.

* * *

Robert was lucky enough to have a guide or mentor like Bill. But not everyone one of us is as fortunate as Robert is.

Today Robert runs a successful Sales Training company. Robert has a diverse team of executives and has created a brand for himself. His company offers Corporate Sales Training programs for midsize companies. And guess what? His audiences are not the college graduates that he initially thought/explained to Bill. His company offers training programs to mid-career Sales executives, who would like to grow in their career.

Where to start and how to start are always questions that are in the minds of many of us, who aspire to become entrepreneurs. We tend to have fear of failure, of success, of what our family will think, what if…questions just do not stop in our mind. Especially when in mid-career where the family has just started and career is going good, starting a new business looks extra risky.

Coming to the question of 'where to start?' There is never a defined time or date when someone decides to start his/her journey. It always starts with your thought followed by the action in that direction.

Ms. Vidya Vellala, Founder & CEO of Evaya Desk says— "The seed of entrepreneurship can start with a small idea or goal in mind. The journey is of evolution. Your idea evolves as you move ahead in your life pursuing your dream. It is a journey that everyone should enjoy."

Vidya Vellala started off on her journey of entrepreneurship, after having worked in the corporate for almost eight-plus years. On being asked how she felt when she first started off, she says, "I had a small idea when I first started. However, I seeded the idea and started building on it. It was an everyday-learning for me. I was a passionate student who would wake up with a new energy to learn. As I continued to learn, my idea kept evolving. By the time I exited Evaya Desk, we had 73% more customers than we had projected three years earlier"

She suggests, "Entrepreneurship is a journey that starts with one step. Take a plunge and never give up on learning."

Taking a plunge into business after working in the corporate world is a bold decision. Based on the type of risk appetite, there are four types of personality traits we see, who set off on their entrepreneurial journey:

a. Dashers - Do not do anything
b. Takers
c. Aversers
d. Mitigators.

Dashers, typically start their entrepreneurial journey because of the following reasons:

- Family pressure.
- Got an opportunity just to take care of an existing business.
- They do not have to do anything.

People carrying this personality trait prefer to work on an established vision or purpose. They follow their instincts and stick with them for a long time. They would wait long enough to take decisions. They are typically scared to admit to the world that things did not work. Rule out going back to work or making any changes to their existing business model. Prefer to stick around doing nothing. Mostly end up blaming markets, people or processes that are stopping their progress.

Risk takers are those who are mostly impulsive decision-makers. They take quick decisions in life and business. They take a plunge into business as soon as they get an idea about a product or service. However, sometimes they are cautious to understand that if something goes wrong, they can always rely on their previous work experience and go back to work. Typically risk takers take calculated risks with a backup plan.

Aversers always want to stay in their comfort zone. They hardly take a step ahead. They feel comfortable sitting and talking to people about starting their own business or venture but never actually take any action. Aversers listen to their inner chatter, which always warns them against taking a risk. They typically surrender to that inner voice and never take action. But they show a lot of enthusiasm when it comes to startup discussions. You may come across aversers in every walk of your life, who enjoy giving free suggestions to everyone and have never started up on their own.

Risk mitigators take every step cautiously. They have the information and know-how to implement things. They start well ahead. They test the waters. They set up a team while they are on a job, working for someone else. They slowly enter the market and understand how things work. As they see things moving in the right direction, they take the leap.

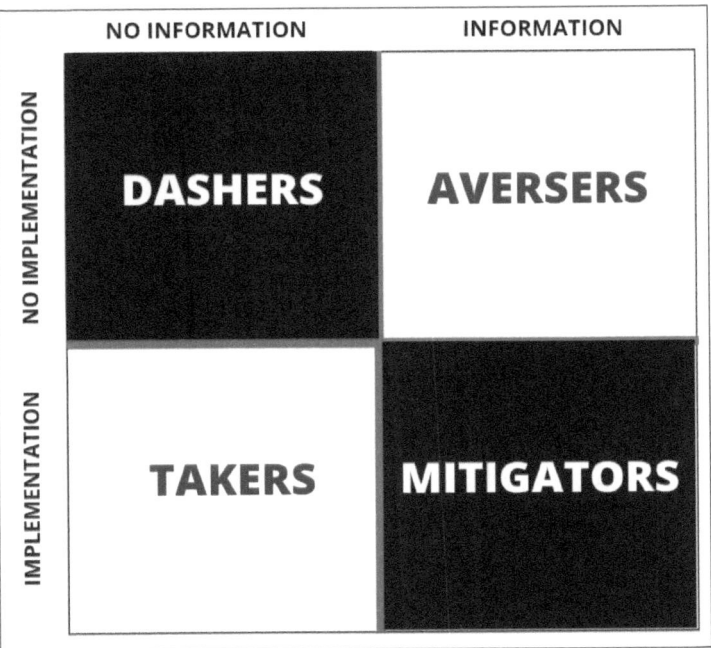

You must have identified yourself as falling into one of the four categories. Congratulations!

Whatever may be your risk appetite in business, you have to start with the following:

1. Decide on your product or service.
2. Identify your target market and where you can find them.
3. Do enough market research and competitor analysis.
4. Understand if you can scale your product or service.
5. Have a future roadmap of your product/service. This need not be clear from day-one, but you should know where you want to travel to.

6. Have an objective in mind. It is not necessary that you have to have a clear objective from day-one. You will evolve. Be a student of life. Keep learning every day.

Now that you have identified the above, you must be wondering: how to start?

Starting up your business, you need minimum paperwork to be done, like your firm/company name, your company registration, your bank accounts, etc. Hire a good CPA/CA who can help you with all this initial setup.

Here are the seven important pillars of any business:

1. Product or Service
2. Marketing
3. Sales & Customer Service
4. Operations & HR
5. Accounting & Finance
6. R & D
7. Management

Do not worry about all these pillars from day-one. You have to be eventually prepared if you are looking to build a multi-million dollar company. However, the essential ones are People, Product and Process.

As an entrepreneur, you must be aware of all these pillars and should have a basic idea of what each pillar is all about. But as you grow, make sure you are establishing the pillars to take care of your business.

* * *

Choosing the Right Partner

Entrepreneurs face another important challenge. When you want to start, you have a question "Should I start alone?" "Should I get a partner?" "Whom to choose as a partner?". Apart from these questions, you may also have a lot of 'if's and but's'. That is completely normal. Every person goes through it. However, it is always wise to choose a person whom you know for a long time and who shares the same passion as you do. Trust me, it could be difficult to find such a person quickly. But keep looking out.

It is not necessary to have your partner ready from day-one. Or this should not be a reason for you to not start up. There are many aspiring entrepreneurs who say, "I am looking for the right partner to start my own business." And unfortunately, they never get started.

How to Identify the Right Partner?

Any relationship, be it in business or in life, builds and stands on "Trust". Finding the right partner hence is always challenging, as it is difficult to trust someone unless you have closely worked together and shared similar experiences in the past.

Many aspiring entrepreneurs who were in their mid-career asked me "how to find a perfect partner for business?" My first suggestion to many people was to discuss their business idea with their life partner, who might be interested to become your partner in your business as well. And trust me, it has worked for many. However, a few aspirants were doubtful and a few were hesitant and a few wrote it off saying "He/She will not be interested and I know!"

When insisted, those people came out with a result. And guess what? Their partners in life became their business partners too. They became successful in setting up their own business and were quickly learning the basics of starting up. As they worked together, they found that their partners were complementing their skills which were absent in the aspiring entrepreneurs.

If your partner is not ready, then look for someone outside.

When asked, Ms. Vidya Vellala says "A partner in business should have the skills that you are not strong at." She continues "If you are strong in technology, delivery and operations and you do not have much knowledge about Marketing and Sales, then choose a partner who can complement for Marketing and Sales."

Sometimes you might have to partner with multiple individuals to complement your skills. Partnering with people having the same skill-set as yours may not help the business, as you both will end up having the same questions.

Key Takeaways

1. There is no good time or bad time to startup. All you need is a commitment to your dream.
2. Have the knowledge of seven pillars. Make it a point to have People, Process and Product in place, before starting up.
3. Find partners who have complementing skills.
4. Understand your personality trait and correct it, if needed, to proceed further.
5. Never give up on your idea. There is nothing called a Good Idea or Bad Idea. Execution is all that makes the difference between success and failure.

※ ※ ※

Chapter 3
MARKETING "THE IGNORED PILLAR"

A Big Differentiator Between Success and Survival
Marketing
Going back to Robert's story on how he started up. Though he knew he was taking a risk by quitting a lucrative career, that was secure and giving him a monthly paycheck, he took the first step.

Six months after he met Bill at his home, Robert started working up all the questions that Bill had asked. He worked on his material for training, identified his paying customers, understood the importance of cash-flows and how to scale up his business. He had a great plan by the end of six months. Though it was vague, he knew he might have to make a few changes to his plan as he moved ahead.

The first thing he did was to register his business as a Sole Proprietorship. He set up all the paperwork, had a team who could prepare the training materials. He got his website developed. Everything seemed perfectly fine to get started.

He started with his own network, reaching out to friends like Bill, and those in authoritative positions in midsize organizations. Though most of them knew Robert well, they never referred him to their organizations.

And six months down the line, he ended up having two-three customers. He was confused about what was not working. He did not know what to do. He felt it was time to have a checkpoint. He went back to his blackboard and started writing down each case, his approach, what went next, and the follow-ups, and then a NO. He derived at a pattern. He realized, he was not talking to the right decision-makers. It was an eye-opening moment for him. Here is a list of things he realized:

- Not reaching decision-makers.
- He ended up spending more time with the low-rank officers, answering their questions and could be losing a lot of prospecting time.
- However, when he reached out to decision-makers directly, he was able to save time with just a YES or a NO answer.

Robert realized he was fishing on the wrong side of the pond. He was prepared to make a few changes in his schedules and start learning from his experiences.

He noted that identifying the right decision-makers and save his productive time were the areas he needed to improve on. He also made a note of the prospects, who were not decision-makers, but still were a channel to reach the decision-makers. So, he hired Susan and shadow trained her on prospecting.

Susan was Robert's friend. They met through one of their common friends three years ago. Susan was working in Sales and carried good experience in closing the leads. Robert felt she would be a good fit to shadow him on the prospecting part.

Laura was watching closely how Robert was taking up things. She was amazed at the transformation that Robert was undergoing as well. She saw Robert becoming more disciplined, his tone changed, he was evolving and growing. Laura was happy with the changes happening with Robert in her life.

By the end of his first year into business, Robert was filing his taxes for the company. There was a lot of paperwork that he was doing along with his CPA. He realized that his business had just made a meager profit. It was a comforting moment for Robert.

However, as he looked at his business for the last six months, he realized that he was still not doing enough. He reached out to Bill again to share his learnings and ask for his feedback.

It was in April, and Bill was in Seattle, busy with setting up his new branch office. He was very happy to hear from Robert. Bill was sure, Robert would make it big in business. To Bill's surprise, Robert conveyed that he was in fact missing something in his business. Bill suggested, if they could discuss at leisure over the weekend. Robert agreed and asked if he could meet Bill in-person in Seattle. Bill was happy to host Robert and they both agreed to meet at Bill's new office.

Robert never visited Seattle before. He wanted to utilize his weekend time perfectly to craft his future roadmap. As soon as he arrived at the airport, he quickly grabbed a bite, booked a taxi and reached Bill's office around 9:45 A.M PST. Bill was waiting for Robert at his office and was excited to meet him.

They exchanged casual pleasantries and Bill walked Robert through his new office. Robert was amazed at the way Bill was taking on his business. Robert was always inspired by the way Bill was growing.

After a few minutes, they decided to get into the brainstorming part of the business. Robert asked a lot of questions regarding his approach, his understanding, what went right and what went wrong, where to stop, where to start, etc.

Bill was a giver of sorts. He always wanted to share his knowledge and experiences in business. He found a perfect student in Robert, who was always curious, willing to learn and grow.

Bill listened to all the questions that Robert asked and said, "Robert, I appreciate you for taking the first step into business. Trust me, you are doing wonderfully well. But, there are a few things many entrepreneurs and business owners don't realize."

Bill asked Robert, "I would want you to list all your employees and what they do on the whiteboard."

Robert did not understand why Bill was asking this question. He felt it was irrelevant. But he did not contradict. He wrote the names of his six team members, their roles, responsibilities and their experience.

Bill continued, "Good! Now write down how you see yourself in the next five years. Make sure your statement is very specific to what type of clients you want to attract."

Robert wrote down "I want to see myself as a successful entrepreneur. I would like to establish myself as the best Sales trainer for automotive Sales teams. My niche is automotive Sales. I would like to work with automotive dealers and distributors to help their organization improve on their monthly Sales. I specifically want to work with dealers selling high-end cars like Porsche, Tesla, BMW and Mercedes."

Bill walked to the board and asked Robert, "Do you think your current team is matching up to the vision you have?"

Robert replied: "Yes."

Bill: "Do you think, your current team is enough to reach your prospects?"

Robert answered: "No"

Bill asked: "What was your budget for Marketing?"

Robert replied: "I have not invested in Marketing. I am working mostly on the referrals from my network."

Bill suggested: "Did you think of Marketing as one of the important aspects of your business?"

Robert replied: "Yes, I have thought about it. But I was not sure if that would work for me?"

Bill: "Advertising, Marketing and Promotions help you promote your business and become a brand. It is something you should never ignore."

Bill had himself spent millions of dollars in the last six years on Marketing. He was now working on building his personal brand as an authority in the market.

Bill asked, "Robert, what do you think about Marketing for your business?"

Robert said, "Marketing is a spend. I feel it is like a black hole where money just disappears."

Bill couldn't hold his thoughts and asked immediately, "Why do you think so?"

Robert replied, "When I was working at the car company, selling cars, I was going through their Marketing budgets. I felt, my company was spending a lot on Marketing, while it was we Salespeople, who were bringing that money back to the company. I felt it was a drain of money."

Bill realized Robert's Marketing blueprint was not right. He explained to Robert that his view on Marketing as a spend needs to be corrected.

Robert was confused. He said, "No Bill, that's what I have noticed my entire life. Hence, I trusted my own network than Marketing my business"

Bill wanted to continue and explain but realized that Robert came from a Sales background. Showing something in numbers would make more sense to him and help him understand more.

Bill quickly drew a chart.

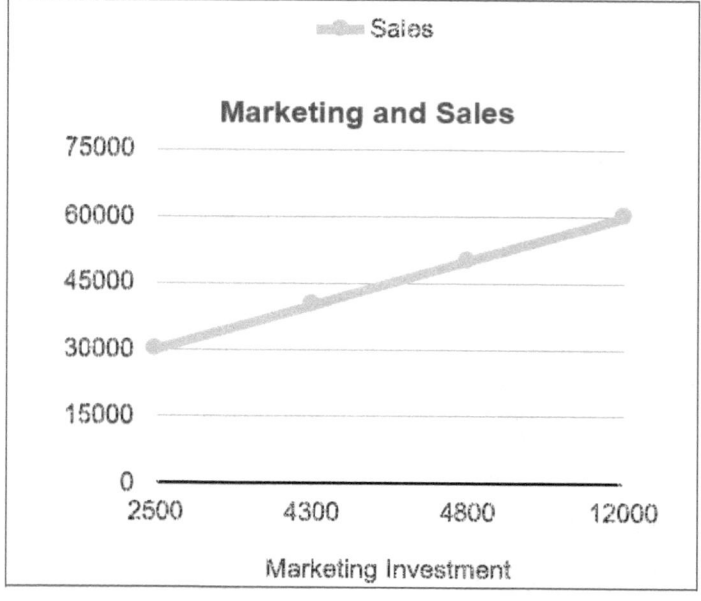

"Robert, what do you infer from this chart?" Bill asked.

Robert argued "Bill, Marketing is a spend. Why are you mentioning it as an investment?"

Bill replied "Robert, my friend, this is where most of the businesses fail to realize the importance of Marketing. They consider Marketing as a spend. When you consider it so, you end up spending it. As you mentioned, it will be just like putting your money in the never-ending blackholes."

Robert was confused. He asked "How do you see it as an investment, Bill? Like my company, I think I will end up spending all, with nothing coming in?"

Bill took a deep sigh. He explained the beauty of Marketing and encouraged Robert to see Marketing as an investment.

Bill continued, "Robert, let me ask you a question. You bought a Tesla high-end model car. You wanted to tell the world around you that you have the costliest car. But after you bought it, you kept it in a garage and never took it out. You thought people will just come to know. Now, tell me, do people really know you have a Tesla Car when they have never seen it?"

Robert replied "No. Never will they know until they see it."

Bill said "That's exactly what business owners do. They spend all their financial resources on building their business or the product or service. Then they are scared of Marketing it or they don't have enough budgets to market it."

"Let me tell you from the customer's standpoint" Bill continued. "John is looking for a solution that solves his problem. You have the solution but, you are not visible in the market. You do not tell anyone that you have a solution. The only few people who know about your product is your team who built it." Robert was listening carefully.

Bill continued, "John searches for a solution online with different keywords. He spends a lot of time searching for it in his network, forums, support groups and everywhere possible. But he doesn't find an answer to his problem."

Bill asked, "Robert, do you see the gap between the customer and the solution? Marketing bridges the gap between them."

Robert realized the importance of Marketing even in his Sales business. As he arrived back in his office, the first thing he did was, to ask his team to start searching for an online Marketing agency. Since he did not have much knowledge of Marketing, he outsourced Marketing activities to one of the agencies in Detroit.

Many entrepreneurs still see Marketing as a spend. While traditional Marketing includes billboards, hoardings, theater advertising, newspaper advertising, etc., today the market share is distributed to included digital Marketing as well.

If you also think that Marketing is a spend and did not yield any results, here are a few reasons why you are thinking so:

1. You did not follow the right Marketing strategy.
2. You did not identify who your target audience is.
3. You ended up with the wrong agency for your Marketing needs.
4. Your Marketing team is not clear with the objectives.

Many business owners end up with a failure at Marketing. It is just a pack of cards falling down, if Marketing goes down the drain.

Here is the impact:

Marketing —> Sales —> Revenue Growth

If Marketing goes wrong, you will not see enough Sales. Not enough sales leads to No Revenue/No Growth.

Why do Marketing activities usually go wrong?

In my first product, when we developed the FALCON product, we found that we had done the following mistakes with regard to Marketing:

1. We knew our target audiences were stockbrokers, specifically those who were starting up. But we did not know where to find them.
2. Our end customers were not tech-savvy to search online for our product.
3. We relied mostly on Digital Marketing, but our customers were not online.
4. We invested in Marketing, but it was not strategic.
5. We had hired only one person, whom we assumed would take care of all the Marketing activities. It was completely a wrong assumption. Marketing is a teamwork.
6. Did not have enough touchpoints to trigger Sales.

These revelations did not happen all at once. As we continued our journey, we realized these one by one. Then we did our course-correction and ensured we did not repeat the mistakes as we moved ahead.

When we started with our SaaS products and services again, we hired a team of Marketing experts, graphic designers, content writers and SEO specialists. Since our products were mostly into SaaS, we identified that outdoor advertising and Marketing are not the right strategies. We slowly strengthened our foot-hold on Marketing. We reached markets across the globe through content Marketing, e-mail Marketing, SEO and Social Media Marketing.

As we unlocked the science of Marketing, we were recognized among our peers. Many of our friends requested us to take up their Marketing projects for their companies. Today we not only market our own products, but also help other businesses with their Marketing requirements. Today we compete with some of the top digital Marketing service companies in the world.

But will Marketing alone help your business grow? Absolutely not!

Marketing gives you a pipeline of clients. You need an essentially strong Sales team who can nudge the clients to make the deals. Marketing and sales are usually perceived to be at loggerheads. But when both work in collaboration, that is when the wonders happen.

Key Takeaways

1. Marketing is an investment.
2. Have a Marketing strategy for your business.
3. Hiring a Marketing team or outsourcing your Marketing division would help you be visible in the market.
4. Always stay visible to the market.

"Out of Sight, Out of Mind". This is true even in this digital world!

* * *

Chapter 4
SALES – TREASURE CHEST OF YOUR BUSINESS

Sales

Erik owns a software training business. They give training in Artificial Intelligence and machine learning for mid-career engineers. He had a very good setup in terms of the classroom and virtual trainings. Most of the virtual trainings were happening over the weekdays in the early morning hours. It was basically focused on working professionals who would want to move to the next level or wanted to switch their existing careers to Artificial Intelligence, Deep Learning and Machine Learning careers.

They hired a Marketing agency. Their expectations were high, unmatched by their Marketing investments. Before they started with digital Marketing, their initial course enrollments were at ten-twelve students per week. They had 50% of those students walking in for the demo classes. And as they started off with their Marketing investment, they saw a close-to-85% increase in their enrollments. But the number of students who attended their sessions was low. They saw less than 10% of the enrolled students turning up for the demo sessions.

When we analyzed their Marketing and Sales funnel, we realized that there was a huge gap in the funnel. Once a student enrolled for a course, there was no Sales process that would trigger. There was no nudging of the leads, no Sales process in place. Students who enrolled over the weekend forgot about the enrollment.

We streamlined their Sales process. We added e-mail templates to their Sales process, that would nudge the students till their demo session was done. These students were further added to the newsletter funnel, where they would be sent interesting articles on AI/ML and Machine Learning, a few case studies that the prospects could relate to, etc.

Once the Sales process was in place, they got a good percentage of students who signed up for their online courses and in-person trainings.

There is a thin line of difference between Marketing and Sales that many business owners fail to understand. Perhaps the leads generated through Marketing may not be something that the Sales team would be ready to work on.

> *"The difference between marketing and sales is that marketing owns the message and sales owns the relationship"*
>
> *– John Jantsch*

What Are Marketing Leads?
Leads that fall into the bracket of potential customers can be categorized as Marketing Leads. These leads are to be nurtured through e-mail Marketing, social media Marketing, etc. and kept engaged with the content. These leads qualify to become Sales Leads when they are ready to buy. That is when these

leads are handed over to the Sales team who closely work with them into registrations, payments, onboarding, etc.

What Are Sales Leads?

Those leads that are ready to pay for your product or service become your Sales Leads.

We see the distinctions clearly in B2B2C platforms like Uber, Zomato, Swiggy, DoorDash, etc. They work on Sales Leads while B2B platforms like Salesforce, Tally or B2C stores, Trainers, Coaches, etc. work on the Marketing Leads model.

As I always say, Marketing and Sales are two important pillars of any business. So are the leads they deal with

In Erik's scenario, the leads generated were a combination of Marketing and Sales leads initially. As they started adding more and more value to their students, they had to spend less and less amount of time and money on the Marketing Leads. Today more than 43% of their business comes from referrals.

Sales is not about selling, it is all about solving.

Confused?

Yes, I believe when you sell something, you are solving a problem for someone. The beauty of Sales is, it gives you an opportunity to understand another person's problem and help them solve it. Now the solution could be solving the problem by giving them a matchstick to light their candle or it could be an application development or it could be as big as building a rocket. Finally, as a Salesperson, we get to solve a problem for our clients. Remember sales is not always about making money. It is all about building relationships and solving. Money will follow, when you solve well for the problems on hand.

When it comes to B2B Sales, we have to narrow down our audience and prioritize. This happens when we carefully understand their problems.

Many people in B2B Sales do the same mistake I did. We tend to speak with the wrong people and get disappointed, as nothing moves forward. We exhaust all our energies answering questions of the wrong people.

The primary focus in B2B Sales is identifying your customer persona with:

M – Money

A – Authority

N – Need

Defining your customer persona and behavior is as important in Sales as in Marketing. It gives you an opportunity to understand their need and solve their problem.

In the previous chapter, if we take the story of Robert, he solves problems for high-end car dealers by training their Sales teams. Now, do you remember, Robert in his first conversation with Bill identified his audience as fresh college pass-outs? Then he realized they did not fall into the MAN persona. The students had the Authority and Need, but they would not have enough money to take up Robert's training classes.

So Robert chose mid-career Sales professionals as one of his target audiences. If we analyze them with MAN criteria, here is what we find:

M-Money – Mid-career professionals are an earning audience. So they can invest in learning from Robert.

A – Authority – These career professionals do not have to wait for someone's approval to take a decision on the training. They have the authority to make decisions about their careers/trainings.

N – Need – Mid-career professionals always look up to move to the next level. To take their career advancement, they should work on improving their skills and closing the deals. Hence they have a tremendous need for up-skills, which Robert provides.

Hence mid-career professionals fall into the right audience for Robert.

Associating himself with car dealers of high-end cars gives Robert an opportunity to fish in the right pond. Hence he made car dealers of high-end cars his primary audience.

> "Great Salespeople are relationship builders who provide value and help their customers win."
>
> – Jeffery Gitomer

Sales Process:

Here is a seven-step process for Sales:

1. Prospecting – Defining your customer persona. Apply the MAN Technique.
2. Connecting – Connect with the personas who fall under MAN Technique, satisfying all the three criteria.
3. Understanding your prospect's needs – Understand their needs and see if your product/service can offer the solution.

4. Proposing a solution – Propose a solution. Sometimes this can be a five-step solution or one-stop solution. Depends on the complexity of the need.
5. Handling Objections – Handle objections and answer any questions the customer may have.
6. Closing the deal – Close the deal which could include delivery/installation or deployment.
7. Repeat, Follow-up or Referrals – Take testimonials, ask for referrals and check with them to see if you can solve any other problems for them.

Typically many Sales processes define qualifying and disqualifying leads as a second step, before connecting. However, it may happen at any of the stages before closing the deal.

Qualifying and disqualifying a lead can happen at any of the first five stages.

Let me briefly explain each of the stages, so you are aware of the Sales process.

PROSPECTING: Looking for leads who map your customer persona. Usually prospecting starts when you define your customer persona and start sending them campaign e-mails or text messages. So the first step before you start prospecting is identifying your customer persona.

With digital transformation, the lines between Marketing and sSles become blurred. Most of the digital Sales funnels are efficient and lead to Sales. With the advent of e-commerce platforms, selling has become less cumbersome. Some online businesses need lesser Sales steps to achieve their revenue goals than other businesses.

FAQs

How should I define my customer persona?

Ask yourself the following questions:

1. What is my product solving?
2. Who are the people who are facing this problem?
3. What is their age?
4. What is their gender?
5. What are their interests and hobbies?
6. What are their behaviors?

Let us take an example of the B2C segment. A top clothing brand defines its customer persona as follows:

Name:

Age: 27 years

Gender: Female

Status: Single

Occupation: Digital Content Manager

Hobbies: Reads Fashion and Lifestyle Blogs, spends most of her time with friends—Shopping, movies, bowling, etc.

Behavior: Social media savvy. Posts regularly on social media and tags her friends, likes staying healthy and vegetarian.

Having defined your customer personas in this detail, your target audience becomes quite narrowed down. You know the exact audience you want to target. When you know whom to target, you also know where to find them—digitally and physically.

Let us take the example of a B2B segment, identifying the personas.

I have this question, "When it comes to B2B, how can we identify a persona, when what we are dealing with is an organization?"

One of my mentors told me—Any segment be it B2B or B2C, there is a person behind, there is an emotional human being making a decision for that organization. You need to identify the persona, feelings, emotions and write them down.

For e.g., you would like to get in touch with the purchase manager in F & B industry, where you would like to be one of the vendors to them. Typical persona could be something like this:

Age: 30-45 years age

Experience: 5-15 years in F & B industry

Occupation: Purchase Head/Purchase Manager

Gender: Male

Interests: Movies, Shopping, Pets, Import/Export Quality

Hobbies: Exploring new products, reading quality-related blogs

Professional Associations: Agricultural Groups, AgroTech

His day could be something where he has to onboard vendors who have approved quality certificates and has targets set every month. He finds very less vendors who suit their F&B needs. At the end of the day, he is disappointed, as he is unable to onboard the right vendors. He did not see vendors like you who have all the criteria met and ready to be on-boarded.

Hence identifying a prospect persona, gives you an immense opportunity to reach the exact target audience.

CONNECTING: When you have prospected your target audience, create the right anchors to connect with them. It could be an engaging e-mail or it could be a follow-up phone call or even scheduling an in-person meeting.

I see connecting as building rapport with your prospects. Many businesses follow this through sending follow-up e-mails before setting up an in-person meeting. The aim of follow-up e-mails to the prospects is to get them familiarized with your products or services. It is all about educating them about what problems you have solved for other businesses with similar personas. Including case studies or white papers would be a good idea to educate your prospects.

When anchored well, you will see that the prospect will come back with a problem statement that he/she would like to discuss with you, which typically leads to a face-to-face meeting or a teleconference.

Common Mistakes Done

Many people in Sales do not understand the power of connecting and anchoring. They tend to send messages like these, which annoys the prospect and makes them keep the Salespeople at bay:

"Hi Prashanthi,
Thanks for connecting with me.
I am xxxx, with XYZ Inc.

We are a team of xx DevOps and CloudOps experts based in Toronto, Canada with extensive expertise in DevOps,

CloudOps, SysOps and TechOps. We are pretty good at CICD Pipelines, Infrastructure as Code, Build Automation, Continuous Deployment, Cloud Automation and Containerization. We have on our team experts in DevOps Tools and certified in Azure and AWS, including security.

I would like to discuss more and explain the value add we can do, if you can give thirty mins.

Thanks, xxxx"

Training the Sales team with do's and don'ts in social media, can really help businesses build the right audience.

UNDERSTANDING YOUR PROSPECT'S NEEDS: Once a prospect agrees to meet with you in-person, you can consider it as the first milestone in the Sales process. It is an opportunity for you to learn, understand and offer a solution to the customer. The solution may not arrive right there at the table. It may arrive after a few subsequent meetings. However, never leave the anchor.

Some people tend to mess up in-person meetings, by going unprepared. Some go overprepared and things get messed up.

Point to Remember: A person who asks the right questions is in control of the conversation.

Many mistake this point as talking, talking and talking. Unfortunately that is incorrect. Sometimes Salespeople keep talking so much that they fail in many aspects. Predominantly the following:

- Lose focus.
- Fail to understand the customer's problem statement.
- Go into too many assumptions.
- Talk/boast about their products and services more.

Finally, they lose the prospects because their problem was never understood.

In-person conversations are the most critical and sometimes decisive ones when it comes to taking an association to the next level. Unfortunately, many business owners and Sales teams tend to ignore this part.

How should one be prepared, for the in-person meeting or a virtual one-to-one meeting?

The first rule to follow when you are going to meet your warm prospect is to do a KYC—Know Your Customer.

What should you know about your customer?
- ✓ Know their job profile. What did they do, how did they start their journey? Which companies have they worked for? Where did they do their graduation? Do they have any recommendations? Did they give any recommendations?
- ✓ Know their social profile. What are their interests, hobbies, behaviors, etc.?

Why should you know these things about your customers?

As I said earlier, one-to-one meetings are the best opportunities to build relationships. And we do not build relationships logically. Relationships are always built on emotional anchors.
- ✓ Try to research about their pain points. These pain points could be at the company level or department level. There is less likelihood of companies revealing their pain points online. However, you could find pain points in the customer reviews, employee reviews, etc. This adds valuable information for you when you want to build relationships and understand their pain points.

- ✓ Point to remember: Never offer solutions in the first face-to-face meetings. This meeting is an opportunity to only ask questions and understand your prospect's problem statements. Your probability of solving the problem could be very less and may end up offering an incorrect solution in the first meeting.
- ✓ Take the problem statement to your team and discuss the very options for solving it. Sometimes your team may ask you some more questions to understand the problem statement in detail. You may have to reach out to your prospect a few more times, before proposing a solution. Hence it is better to set a clear expectation before you conclude your first meeting. Ask your prospect for the following:
  - Can I reach you in case my team needs more clarifications? Or can you assign a single point of contact whom we can reach out to?
  - What is the best mode to reach out—Mobile, E-mail or other channels?
- ✓ Keep your prospect engaged till you find a solution.

PROPOSING A SOLUTION: As indicated earlier, usually it takes some time to analyze the problems and come up with a solution. It is preferable to come up with at least three different solutions, before presenting "THE ONE" solution to your customers.

When you have to present a solution, never send it via e-mail. There is a high chance that your customer does not understand your proposal. Hence I recommend you invite them for a walkthrough of the solutions.

Present the three solutions and give your proposition. Giving proper logical reasons to narrow down on "The One" solution will not only help your prospect understand your depth of understanding, but will trust you with the job to be done.

At this point, the prospects usually come to a decision point with a go or no-go.

Many startups in services usually forget one more thing at this point. They forget to disqualify the prospects.

What is prospect disqualification?

Steps to prospect disqualification again fall into the following items:

1. Is the proposed solution understood by the prospect?
2. Does he/she have the required expertise to give the necessary inputs needed to execute the solution?
3. Does he or she understand the life cycle of the project?
4. Do they have the financial bandwidth to accept a contingency proposal, just in case of a delay?

Usually, startups in their initial years are desperate to get new customers on board. They accept to take up a job at a meager cost. This spoils the entire startup ecosystem. And this does no good to the prospect and the startup. They both end up with a sub-standard delivery and sub-standard product.

If the answer to any of the questions above is a NO, then I would suggest re-evaluating your prospect before signing up with them.

Why Should You Qualify or Disqualify a Prospect?

Usually, prospects that do not have the knowledge of execution, tend to give a hard time. Especially if they do not have anyone from their side who understands the language of execution, the project/product/program ends up in a mess.

The reason you should disqualify such prospects is, to save time and effort for you and your team. Some prospects even threaten to sue, or make the vendors responsible, when they do not understand the life cycle. This leads to unnecessary discussions, head-aches and diversions. You tend to lose focus. Qualifying such leads does more harm than good in the longer run.

Handling Objections

After the solution is proposed, the clients may come up with several objections. And the objections could be falling into the following categories:

- ✓ Price Objections: Your prospect may say, the solution is too pricey.
  - Handle: Show them the value, return on investment, saving in terms of time and money, emotional satisfaction when they sign up with you or your product. Tell the prospect about all the reasons other than the solution itself. Show how you can add value to their business.
- ✓ Capability Objections: We are not sure if you can execute this solution. Did you do it for a similar business like ours?
  - Handle: Every business is unique, and the solution is tailor-made for every business. If you have already implemented a similar solution, you can refer to your

approach and how you solved it for your previous client.

✓ Need more time – Your prospect may raise a time objection saying, they need more time to get back to you.

- Handle: Ask them how much time they need to decide, what are the factors they want the time for. Some may say, they are looking for other competitors, they need more time to get the budgets in place, they need to streamline a few processes to get started. Giving them an urgency to close the deal, can make them commit you to the product.
- Some most common ways of handling this objection is giving a time frame to close.

E.g., "This offer is valid only for two days. After two days, I may not be able to guarantee you the same price."

✓ Service Objections: Some prospects may raise a concern about after-Sales support in a few cases—depending on the product/service you sell.

- Handle: Ask your prospect, what kind of support they are looking for. Explain to the customer about your Customer Support and how they are trained to handle any issues. Their availability for the support and the SLAs you have.

  As a Salesperson, you have to be aware of everything that happens after the prospect makes the payment. Hand-hold the prospect, so he/she feels comfortable and confident that they made the right decision. This will help you to reach out to them in the future for any referrals and testimonials. Also helps in building goodwill in the market.

Mistakes: Many sales representatives leave the prospects right after they are handed over to the support team or onboarding team. Customers usually feel dissatisfied, when they do not know whom to reach out to when needed.

Solution: Giving your customer a clear onboarding process and assigning them to a dedicated account manager gives them confidence in the deal they have entered.

- Authority Objection: "I have to discuss with my partners to make a decision." "I need to discuss with my Senior VP to make a decision." These are the typical authority objections we may hear.

Handle: "Can we check with him now? Is he available to discuss today or tomorrow?" are the best questions you can ask when the prospect raises an authority objection. Most of the time, when the decision-maker is available, the deals get closed immediately—with a "Yes" or a "No".

Handling objections not only gives you an opportunity to clear things for your prospect but also to build a relationship with your prospects.

* * *

Chapter 5
CUSTOMER SERVICE

The Overlooked Chapter in Business
Customer Service

While Sales does take care of conversions, good customer service helps you save customer acquisition costs and retain existing customers for a longer time. Today with the world coming narrower with the Internet, Customer Service is not just limited to chats and e-mails. It has extended to social media channels that can build or kill a company's reputation. In some businesses, customer service decides the future of a company as well.

A decade ago, in the early 2010s, deals or a sale offer caught customer's attention. Customers were searching for the best online deals. But today, customer behavior has changed completely. They look at several factors like Sales, reviews, post-sale customer service and support, before making a buying decision. With many competitors online, customers use certain metrics of their own to make a purchase decision. Hence it is important for a company to keep track of their customer ratings, reviews and reputation online.

Here is the story of Arushi, who fell into the risk of losing her business.

Arushi runs her own boutique retail store for women's and kids' wear. She serves her community, friends and family.

She delivered close to 300+ pieces of designer clothes to her customers before she started her own online brand store.

With great difficulty, she convinced her husband and in-laws that she would be able to manage the house and work simultaneously. She had a ten-year-old son and her husband was a Sales Executive in a reputed insurance company.

She got her e-commerce website developed and an online payment gateway integrated. She also hired a Marketing agency to promote her brand online. The first six-to-nine months were very encouraging, as she saw her friends referring to her work, she was taking orders from unknown people and delivering them on time. She had increased her team size from three to twelve. However, after nine months she observed that the number of orders she received were declining.

One night she got so desperate, she wanted to know what was going wrong. She checked her store as any other customer. She went through all the steps that a customer would go through and finally there she was… She missed out on all the reviews that her customers were putting up. She never answered any of the questions that her customers were asking. She was too busy with delivery and operations that she missed out on the important customers. Dissatisfied customers were putting up bad reviews and she hardly noticed that her online reputation was taking a dig. And now after nine-to-ten months, she was left with fewer orders, a bad reputation and risked the business.

As she realized what went wrong, Arushi quickly hired a customer service and customer engagement intern who could take care of all the communications on social media. Today, Arushi runs a successful local brand and has a tribe of her own, who like her collections and order from her on a regular basis.

Customer Service plays a game-changer role for many businesses. Especially when it comes to e-commerce businesses, banking, finance, insurance segments, customer service adds huge value in retention, customer feedback and customer reviews. It gives an opportunity to increase the revenues for the business.

How to Start with Customer Service?

In e-commerce businesses, typically customer service starts right after the customer has placed an order. They might be looking for tracking numbers, might be looking for shipping information, etc. However, most of the e-commerce post-Sales services are automated and customers are kept informed about every stage of their order processing. However, if the e-commerce lifecycle is not automated for post-Sales customer service, the business will be overwhelmed with e-mails, calls and social media queries.

In our experience, we saw many e-commerce businesses still have a separate team for customer service to process any returns, replacement or re-order requests they may receive. Many times customers prefer to talk to humans, than a bot. Hence, customer service still has prominence and the human touch adds value to the business.

> *You must continually increase your learning, the way you think, and the way you approach the organization. I've never forgotten that.*
>
> *– Indra Nooyi*

* * *

Chapter 6
LEADERSHIP

The Essential Pillar of the Business
Leadership

BEING A LEADER:

A leader is someone who is inspired by his/her vision and inspires others to view that vision ahead. For e.g., the vision of Martin Luther King was to have equal rights for all men and that his children would be judged by the character and not the color of their skin. That vision of his, synced with many of his followers, whose demonstrations and protests brought a major change in the US Law and history.

Apple Inc.'s vision to "Make best products on Earth" inspired many people to have a similar vision. Thus Apple became a world leader, inspiring entrepreneurs to think of making not just any product, but products that make life easier for people to use.

In both the cases of Apple and Martin Luther King, neither of them had the power of doing everything all by themselves, but their vision inspired many people. Martin Luther King was not even a lawmaker, but his famous "I have a dream" speech, in August 1963, inspired many. His vision to see America as a land with equal opportunities for everyone, led everyone to take action. This led the reformers to put civil rights on the top of their agenda, thus leading to the passage of the Civil Rights Act in 1964. Leadership is all about inspiring people to see your vision and help them take action.

> *If your actions inspire others to dream more, learn more, do more and become more, you are a leader.*
>
> *– John Quincy Adams*

Joseph started his software services business after having worked in software Sales for a few companies. He had more than ten years' experience in selling SaaS, ERP products. He was married to a beautiful woman Sonya and blessed with two beautiful children Kim and Andrew.

Joseph took a leap of faith and took up business. His objective was to help small businesses adopt the right SaaS Software. Having worked with software product companies directly and having met hundreds of small business owners, he gained the confidence to start on his own.

He collaborated with a couple of his friends, who gave him enough financial support to set up his team and infrastructure. Though he was good at closing the leads, he was not good at delegating the work. He was taking the entire responsibility of delivery all by himself. Initially, when the volume of work was low and he had fewer clients, he was able to manage Sales, delivery and operations with the few resources on hand. He partnered with some software companies who specialized in customizing SaaS and ERP software. These companies would deliver him the work he needed. However, a year-and-a-half into the business, he started losing it all. His vendors stopped responding, his employees started leaving and everything was falling apart.

He pondered over what was going wrong, but unfortunately never figured out anything. He continued to work with different vendors. If a vendor stopped with him, he found another vendor. Finally, clients stopped giving him business as he was not delivering. It was a mystery for Joseph to figure out what went wrong. He discussed this with one of his friends, Matt, who was running a software company and had started much ahead of Joseph. Matt was also one of the vendors for Joseph initially. But like all the other vendors, Matt also stopped with Joseph after a couple of projects. But Matt and Joseph maintained their friendship.

Joseph invited Matt for a meeting in a coffee shop. Joseph was desperate to know why he was failing, and what mistakes he was making. They were scheduled to meet at 4 P.M. on a Sunday.

Joseph had already arrived and was waiting for Matt to join him. Matt was there right at 4 P.M. Having seen Joseph after a period of one year, Matt was very happy and glad to meet his friend. Matt was expecting Joseph to discuss some success stories. Little did Matt know it was the other way round.

Having ordered themselves a cup of coffee, Joseph said, "Hey, Matt, thank you for coming on my request. I am glad to see you after a long time."

Matt replied, "Same here Joseph. So, what's up? How is everything coming along?"

Joseph said, "Look Matt, I have been doing everything well, I hope correctly. But slowly, I started moving on the downside. I am not sure why my clients are backing off. My employees started leaving right after six months."

Joseph continued, "I know it is too late now, but I am really not able to figure out what was going wrong."

Matt acknowledged Joseph's concerns. Matt said, "Joseph, do you know why I never collaborated with you after our first two initial assignments went wrong?"

Joseph replied, "Yeah I remember, we worked on a couple of projects together, but didn't actually think why you didn't work with me after that."

"Thank you for being honest in saying you never thought about it!" Matt replied.

Matt said, "Joseph, the problem is not with you, but the leadership style that you follow."

"After our first two assignments, I figured out that we may not be able to go a long way. So I quit working with you"

Joseph was surprised. He did not understand why!

Joseph asked, "Sorry Matt, I did not realize it. But why did you stop working with me?"

Matt replied "I thought you must have figured out all by now. But looks like you haven't yet, buddy!"

Joe felt shameful. He asked, "Yes, Matt. You are right! I am still looking for answers. Can you please help me over what went wrong in our case?"

Matt replied, "Joe, business is all about building relationships and trust with your employees, vendors and clients. If we miss that, we fall into a delude. And I guess that's what has happened."

Joseph replied "Yeah, I was trying to build and maintain relationships. Not sure, where it went wrong."

Matt explained "Relationships are built on trust, Joe. So when people lose trust, relationships fail. Coming straight to the point, we usually focus on building relationships with clients. We tend to ignore our other relationships with employees, vendors and sometimes family. But when the client leaves, who are you left with?"

Joe said, "It is family and trusted employees."

Matt replied "Yes, you are right! But when we tend to overlook that aspect and give the focus to our clients, that's when things fall apart."

"I am not saying clients are not important. I am saying, employees, vendors and family are equally important," Matt said. "And when you lose any of them the whole equation gets wrong."

Joseph went back and looked at what happened with the projects he worked alongside Matt's team. He realized that he never respected or paid attention to what Matt's team was saying about the delivery and the timelines. He insisted the team do things quickly and never credited them for the work that was done. Joe realized how stupid he was, when it came to acknowledging and respecting the vendor's team and keeping up their morale. He also realized that his payments were not prompt and he kept postponing them for his vendors.

Slowly he started to realize that it was not only with Matt, but most of his vendors had left because of the same reason. It was the same for his employees; he did not keep them motivated for long, hence they left.

Now everything was unfolding in front of Joseph. He realized what mistakes he had committed. He felt depressed and disappointed. He did not know what to do. He took a break from all the chaos. He had two choices left in front of him—To quit, or to start afresh?

He took the opinion of his family. His family insisted to continue pursuing his passion. Joseph's passion was always to set up his own business and help small businesses with the right software. He decided to restart afresh.

This time Joe was more careful in whom he recruited, whom he was working with and building long-term relationships. He made a clear list of things that he was strong at, and things he could delegate. His another big bottleneck was handling finances. He was very bad at it. Hence he decided to delegate them to a trusted partner.

Today Joseph and Matt collaborate on several projects and have built a strong relationship at business and personal levels. They call themselves complementing each other when collaborating on a client's project.

The power of leadership breaks or makes a company. As you saw, Joseph was willing to learn from his mistakes. He was poised to grow.

The first step, you must have noticed, was acceptance of his mistakes and taking responsibility. The second one was learning from the mistakes. Third one was to stay positive and continue the pursuit. These are the three main qualities of a leader.

Leadership is what decides whether an organization is going to run for a longer time or a shorter time. Leadership style either makes or breaks the organization.

Leadership in my life has taught me many things. I have learned how to lead a team, how to stay with the team and how to celebrate with the team.

Many business owners are confused about leadership. They are not sure how to be a leader. Hence they end up either being a coercive leader, forcing their employees to do what they think is right or end up being authoritative, controlling the team.

Leadership I understood is all about taking your team along with you. Leading your way, so you have leaders getting trained under you. Many a time, your teams may not understand that you are trying to make them leaders. But just remember that they are not ready yet.

I am proud to have created few leaders in my journey, who have moved out and performing very well in their own roles. It makes you feel very happy when they credit you for the leadership style you have taught them.

※ ※ ※

Chapter 7
FINANCE AND CASH-FLOWS

The Un-Compromised Pillar

One of the very important reasons many people fear getting into business is—finances. Either they do not know how to handle finances or they have a fear of handling them.

Handling personal finances is never taught in schools and colleges. Hence it becomes a big bottleneck when it comes to handling them in life and business. Having no financial planning ends up with no growth path. The same is true for business as well.

> *"Poor cashflow management is one of the top reasons for a vast proportion of business failures. 70% of the businesses were found profitable, when they closed their doors."*
>
> *– Dryrun.com*

Here are the top five financial aspects that business owners should never overlook:

1. Financial Cash-flows:

   When it comes to defining cash-flows, we only look at either income or expenses. Many operate under the assumptions about cash-flows. Especially looking at only incoming numbers that look good and giving a blind eye to what is going out of the system.

The best way to take control of your company's finances is by making a cash-flow statement for your startup/business. Make sure to go over it every once in a fortnight or a month. Have your accounts and finance teams sit with you to help you understand the various aspects of income and expenses. Remember "What gets measured, gets done." If you have your numbers right, you will be able to stay profitable in the business. In the end business always boils down to the numbers.

2. Look at your fixed costs:

When it comes to our personal lives we add up fixed costs way too casually. For e.g., renting a larger apartment space, where you spend little time at home. And we focus more on wants than on needs. Buying a luxury car ignoring its mileage, buying a full coverage TV Pack, etc. are some of the ways we add up fixed costs in our personal life.

The same goes with business as well. Keep adding more people to the company, where the existing team is having less work or less billing, adding more rental space for the office without having enough cash-flows, etc. After a few months, we realize that we are not catching up with the finances.

Tip—Be aware of your fixed costs. Understand your company's financial health.

3. Planning for financial set back:

Many a time, when businesses run as small teams, they work on razor-thin margins. At the slightest difficulty, they start looking for ways and means to hold the business tight. Especially when it comes to a sudden client withdrawal, a downturn in the markets or like the COVID Pandemic that hit the world. Small businesses that overcame these situations can be assumed to have successfully survived and thrived.

The first sign of a setback, usually leads to some business owners looking at cutting down the teams. That happens because they kept adding more to the fixed costs. However, I would suggest teams to look at other means of saving the costs than cutting short the team.

4. Turning a complete blind eye on finances and leaving it to others:

   For many, financial management is a nightmare. This restricts many from choosing business as their career path. However, for someone who takes the leap of faith and starts his/her business, finances can give sleepless nights. Some business owners try to find partners who complement these skills and some try to outsource this part to the experts. Both the options are good until, you as a business owner are wary of the numbers going on in your organization.

   When it comes to making the right decisions, the financial aspects of your company play a key role. Do not outsource these tasks and turn a blind eye to your company's financial health.

5. Set clear financial goals for your business:

   Business is all about numbers—People, Cash-flows, clients, company value, Marketing spend, investments made, etc. Everything has to do with numbers. Setting clear goals in your business gives you a vision to aim for.

Setting up monthly, quarterly and annual financial goals helps you to stay close with your numbers and focus on achieving them consistently.

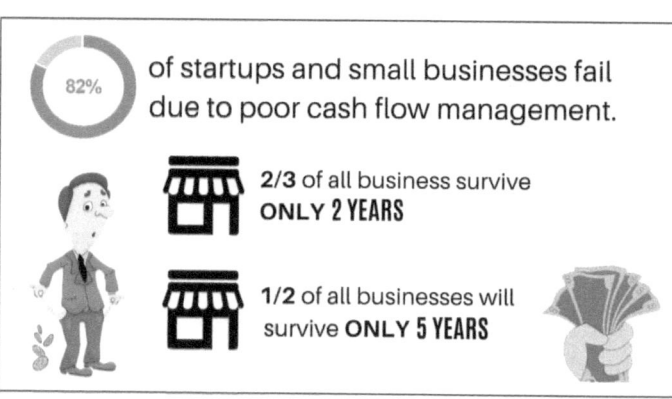

Getting Your Numbers Right

Statistics reveal that half of the small businesses do not survive past five years. Financial mistakes like overestimating Sales, underestimating costs, relying too much on credits have played a major role in these debacles. Financial discipline does indeed play a major role in the success of any organization.

Keep your numbers Right and Ready!

How to generate enough cash-flow?

- Build a vertical to provide services.
- Training.
- Have control on Cash inflows and cash outflows.
- Get all your payments in advance.

- Ensure your delivery model is milestone-wise and you get paid in advance for each milestone.
- Do not be hesitant to say "NO" to services, when they are not generating the cash-flows to keep your team on board.
- Add value to your services than encouraging discounts.
- Preferably have annual subscriptions for your products (if SaaS).
- Control your expenses.
- Use your assets optimally.
- Ensure your fixed costs are in control.

Is Bootstrapping a Good Idea for Your Business?

Bootstrapping is always the way to start with. It has both an emotional and psychological impact on you and your business.

What is Bootstrapping?

Bootstrapping is funding your business with your own cash.

When you bootstrap, you will be careful about what you are spending at and what are the investments in your business. Developing a product is an investment that you make in your business. Unfortunately, many people fail to realize this.

Advantages of bootstrapping:

- You have control over your cash-flows
- You tend to spend carefully and wisely
- When you seek an investor for funding, you will be able to give enough confidence about your investment habits.

Fact is "If you don't trust your product and invest in it initially, how can anyone else trust and invest?"

You will be able to build the confidence in your investors that they are making the right investment with the right team.

* * *

Chapter 8

STAGES OF BUSINESS FROM STARTUP TO SUSTAINABLE

Many businesses start up as soon as they have an idea in mind. The same way we started FALCON. There is nothing wrong with it. Starting up with your own business with an idea is good. But ask yourself, how committed you are toward your business. Are you ready to do whatever it takes to make it successful?

The first thing as you decide to start your business, you have to narrow down whether you would be into a product or service.

Once you have decided on a product or service, here are the first few steps you should take:

1. Write down the problem that you are solving
2. How is your product solving it?
3. Who are your customers?
4. Who are your competitors?
5. What are your competitors offering?
6. What is your USP that can differentiate you from your competitors?

Once you see yourself committed to your startup and business, here are the stages you should be aware of:

- Idea – When we find ourselves with a fantastic idea that we feel can solve in the market, the first thing we do is to research for similar ideas if they are already in the market: if there are other products or services solving the same problem that you felt you could solve. But unfortunately many startup ideas die right there!

  Many startup ideas fail before even launching. They fail at the idea-stage itself. The reasons could be many—do not know how to take the product to the market, research showed that a similar idea failed earlier, inner chatter, low confidence after few days or several external factors.

  Here is what I found in my experience. Science says that an average human being gets thirty-five – forty-eight thoughts per minute. These thoughts could be about past, present, future, or innovations or ideas or mistakes or assumptions and many, many things. They could also be about people, places, things or ideas. And a million people could get the same idea at different times in different parts of the world. But that should not stop you from pursuing an idea.

  Evaluate your idea consistency. Write down the ideas that you get every day. Revisit those ideas every month for the next six months. You will see a pattern. A pattern that tells you which problem you are passionate to solve. And BOOM!!! Start working on that idea, so you will have the answers to all the above questions. And then you are all set to start your business.

  Please note: The above time frame is just indicative. Some people also find their idea consistency in a month or two, but for some it could take as long as six months.

- Product – Product/Service – Define your product or service that will help you solve a problem. Identify your audience and define your customer persona as you read in earlier chapters.
- Product-market fit/Service-Market Fit – Analyze the product/market fit. Some of the ways of doing it are to conduct surveys, send questionnaires or interview your target audience. This will also help you build a story around your product or service.

  It is interesting to hear the story of McDonald's and Ray Kroc's vision for it. Before Ray Kroc saw the vision behind McDonald's he saw the pain in customers. He saw every restaurant and takeaway making the customers wait for a long time to deliver food. Especially for travelers, it was a pain. They had to wait for the food to arrive and then mostly incorrect order was delivered. When he experienced McDonald's he saw something for America. The restaurant that every American family would love. He translated his vision into a reality, as he pursued his dream with persistence.
- Product development – Team, Clients, Roadmap, cash-flows, investments, etc.

  Having a roadmap for your product gives you clarity of thought. It gives you a clear picture as to what resources you need and when you need them. Most of the startups include this in their business plan.

Once the product development roadmap is finalized, you may want to plan the finances, team and timelines. Define MVP and start with product development.

Service Development: This is no different from product development. The only difference is the absence of a product. In service development also, you need to plan for the team, the skills you need, process flow, customer engagement and service closure.

- Marketing & Sales – Strategy and Execution

    Many startups plan a waterfall model of approach when it comes to taking their solution to the market. However, they forget that the audience needs to be engaged even before the product is in the market. Instead of waiting for the product to be out in the marketplace, it is advisable to have your market prepared for the product.

    This strategy is followed by many technology companies including Google and Apple Inc. Apple advertises/releases the new designs to the market to keep alive the curiosity of the target audience. Releasing new features, even before the product gives the target audience enough knowledge to make a purchase decision. This strategy is also followed in real estate. For software products and services also, it is no different.

- Traction – Market acceptance – Be ready to test your product and see traction in the market. Releasing Alpha and Beta versions, gives you a feedback from your market. This not only indicates market acceptance, but also gives you a confidence to go further in the journey.

    This does not mean, if you do not see traction, your product is wrong. No, I do not mean to say that. If you do not see traction, probably you might be selling to the wrong audience. Check your use-cases, go back to the black board and identify the target audience.

Here is the story of one of my friends, who started his own personalized photo gifting store. He was in the business of selling beautiful memories in the form of Mosaic photographs. Having gained enough traction with his brick-and-mortar store, he wanted to give convenience to his audience to place an order with him, instead of walking into the store. He got a mobile App developed for B2C customers and started Marketing it to his target audience.

He was disappointed, as none of his customers were using the mobile App; instead they preferred to walk into the store and place an order. His idea of developing a mobile App for B2C customers was a disaster. He was trying to find the answers to many of his questions. He received his first order through mobile after almost nine months of struggle. And to his surprise, it was an enterprise/corporate order, which was huge. He had to deliver four hundred and fifty-three pieces of personalized gifts to a doctor's community for a Pharmaceutical company.

That moment, he hurriedly went back and looked at his App statistics. He realized that his B2C customers did not need an App, whereas B2B customers needed it, as they would need personalized gifts frequently. When he went to analyze deeper he realized, his B2C customers were placing repeat orders only once in every six months, and to place such an order, they did not want to waste the App real estate on their mobile devices. That was it! Thus he realized, he was perhaps looking into a different direction, while the market was searching for this platform elsewhere.

This is the reality. Many business owners stop looking in the other direction and consider their idea failure. I would say, there is no "BAD IDEA". The way we perceive, execute and take to the market could be wrong. So believe in your idea and pursue it to your best abilities. Sometimes we do not see it the way it is, but other people see it differently and take it. Look for the third eye, take feedback, find a way and move forward.

- Customer service – As described in detail earlier, Customer Service helps you to retain your existing customers, build a goodwill in the market and give you the confidence to pursue your idea further.
- Scaling – Many startups leave it at Customer Service and are content with what has been achieved. However, when the product does not scale to the next level, to solve problems in-depth or across geographies or across various sectors, we may be limiting your product or service potential.

  When it comes to scaling your services, it is essential to have a process in place. The process can be replicated in any geography with minimum cultural changes.
- Success. As I define it, success is the consistency with which we achieve our goals.

A startup may fail in any of the above stages. But the failure is only a perception. Learning from mistakes and moving forward is important in the journey of an entrepreneur. As Ray Kroc, the founder of McDonald's, said "Business is all about persistence"

> *It is always better to underpromise and overdeliver than vice versa. For this one need not break the law of the land.*
> *— N R Narayana Murthy*

* * *

Chapter 9

WHAT SHOULD YOU DO WHEN YOU ARE STUCK?

Many times, as we start, we face many hurdles. And some hurdles keep us stuck in between. We try hard to find ways to move forward, but unfortunately, it takes some time to figure out things.

Andy is a real estate agent who quit his job and started his own agency. He has close to eight years' experience helping customers buy residential properties. But he always had a dream of starting his own business. Family and kids kept him motivated to stay on the job.

But Andy realized, his passion was not aligned with his company's purpose. He had to hard-sell a few properties, that he felt might not be the right fit for his client's needs. He decided to quit and start his own business.

A few days into his business, he tied up with many real estate companies to sell their properties. His mission was aligned with his passion and it kept him motivated to suggest the best properties to his clients. His business was growing. However, he felt stuck at one point. He was not able to grow further. His income was stagnant. His business reached a point where he saw no growth. He felt stuck, disappointed and did not know what to do. He continued to work, but did not know how to take the business to the next level.

In the journey of entrepreneurship, it is natural that one gets stuck at some point like Andy. We either get distracted with multiple things going on, sometimes we do not see enough support from the market, we are unable to increase the company revenues and sometimes the finances are not enough to keep us afloat. This is natural and part of our journey.

Here is a piece of good news. The moment you feel stuck, is the moment you are attracting your solutions. But again it always depends on the mindset and your thoughts. If you are always saying to yourself "I am stuck", "I am stuck" and "I am stuck", you will always stay wherever you are. And you will be stuck there for a long time.

Rather ask yourself the right questions. "What should I do to get to the next level?", "How can it take my business to the next level?" Asking yourself these questions, shows you the way you can move to the next level.

In the case of Andy, he realized, he was stuck. He asked himself, "How can I become like Re/MAX?" "What should I do to compete with the best guys in real estate?" and guess what happened? He started finding answers.

He met his old friend Mike, who was into a different business. Mike referred Andy to growth seminars. Andy then joined a couple of masterclasses. He found a few people whom he could collaborate with. He learned how to set up a team, systems, processes, etc. He started building on top of what he already had. Soon he was competing with the best real estate guys in the town.

When you are stuck at some point, ask yourself the right questions. Keep your antennas open. You may find answers in the form of situations, friends, suggestions, etc. Remember, getting stuck at some point in life and business is normal. Realizing the situation, asking the right questions and finding the answers are the key to overcome that situation. Keep looking out for the answers. Try your best to get out of the "I am Stuck" situation. Probably this is what happened to Ray and Dick in the case of McDonald's. They were stuck with their San Bernardino, CA location. They tried franchises earlier, but did not know how to run. They failed miserably, only to find answers from Ray Kroc, who successfully started more than twelve hundred Franchises of McDonald's across the United States and more than seven hundred franchises across the globe.

> *"Keep the fire inside you alive. Keep looking out for solutions. You will get out of the "stuck" situation, just like magic."*
>
> *– Prashanthi Kolluru*

* * *

Chapter 10
FINDING YOUR WHY?

At the beginning of the book we read the story of John, who could not start his business, Anita who ran the business, but could not have the appetite to go further than eighteen months and Sarit, who continues to be a consultant. What was missing in all these people? Why were they not able to pursue further? They did not define why they wanted to start in the first place.

Everything in this world has a purpose. It is only that we fail to recognize that our life has a purpose and just live by the norms of the society. Some think serving our family is our purpose, some believe they are born for a greater purpose but do not know what it is. Many men and women continue to be blinded by the society, pressures from external sources, etc. They succumb to those forces and pressures. Hence they stay where they are. Here comes the story of a dreamer.

Elizabeth was a little girl with many dreams. She wanted to be a scientist, who can find cures for diseases. She studied and specialized in microbiology. She became a microbiologist working in a lab, doing experiments on microbes and diseases. She was working on carcinogenic cases, where their lab was finding cures for cancer.

She loved her job and felt she was living her life of dreams and purpose. She was happily married to Matt. They had two beautiful kids, Ashley and Sean.

Ashley and Sean were growing up quickly. Matt was working as an engineer for a construction company. He was a passionate engineer who wanted to build engineering marvels. Matt leaves for office after dropping Ashley and Sean at their school.

It was mid-summer; as Matt was getting ready to the office, he suddenly collapsed in the kitchen. Elizabeth did not know what to do. She made an emergency call to the hospital. An ambulance arrived and took Matt to the nearest hospital. Elizabeth was worried. She dropped the kids at school and followed to Matt's hospital. She did not want the kids to be worried.

The doctors ran many tests for Matt. Finally they got a report that Matt was suffering from early-stage cancer. It was affecting his kidneys. Since it was in an early stage, there was not any immediate threat. However, the disease was not curable by itself. It did not have any cure or medicines. The only thing the doctors could do was to prevent the spread to other parts of the body. They prescribed a few medicines and discharged him from the hospital.

Being a microbiologist herself, Elizabeth understood the case. She was already working on few carcinogenic cases in her lab, which gave her an opportunity to study the cancer-causing microbes that affect the kidneys.

She quickly made a proposal with her higher-ups to work on these microbes. Her request was turned down. The reason given was—they had to queue up the item as their budgets were already assigned to the existing research. However, she persuaded her manager and offered to work a few hours after the office, to study these microbes. But to no avail.

She was disappointed. She was feeling that the dream that she had, to become a scientist and find a cure for diseases was not aligned with where she was working and what she was doing. She saw her dreams shattered and the irony that she was not able to help her husband, but see him die was more painstaking. She could not discuss this with Matt, as it would not help him in any way. After thinking for many days, she decided she would talk to one of her cousins, who was also a microbiologist and working in the same field. Elizabeth immediately called-up her cousin Daisy.

Daisy was working with a Disease Prevention Lab for quite some time. In fact, Daisy's passion for working on diseases and finding cures is what inspired Elizabeth also to tread the same path. Daisy was eight years older than Elizabeth and had gained a good reputation in the microbiologist community. She was well-known for her research on brain cells.

It was the beginning of fall and a Friday. Daisy was busy making weekend plans for her family. She was very excited, as it was a long weekend. Her phone was buzzing. She immediately picked up the call, it was Elizabeth. She was very happy to hear from Elizabeth after a long time. But she soon realized Elizabeth was calling for help. Daisy offered to meet her over the weekend.

Elizabeth and Daisy met at a mall over the weekend. Daisy was shocked to see Elizabeth. She had lost her bubbly face, looked sleep-deprived and weak. Daisy asked her if everything was okay. Beth told her about everything that was happening in her life and how she was not able to help her husband. Beth was sure she could find a cure, but she was not able to leverage the expertise she had, and was looking for some help and support.

Daisy asked, "Beth, what's going on. What are you thinking right now?"

Beth replied, "Daisy, I have been working with this lab for quite some time. But somehow, my life's purpose does not seem to align with theirs. I cannot work with passion, when my hands are tied up with bureaucratic budgets and procedures."

Daisy replied, "I am listening."

Beth continued, "I would like to open up my own lab and dedicate the research to only cancer and carcinogenic cases. I wanted to take your opinion."

Daisy was very happy to hear that. She assured her it was a good decision and would support her as much as possible.

Today Beth's cancer lab has not only found the cure for Matt's disease, but helped millions of families survive cancer. They are much recognized in the healthcare community and continue to inspire millions of entrepreneurs. She has a special team, that works only on rare kinds of cancer-causing microbes. And they do not queue up their research, but prioritize them up based on the severity and life-expectancy.

As was the case with Beth, she had a "Why", but that "Why" strengthened, when she wanted to help Matt and millions of people like her, who were suffering like Matt.

The important characteristics of charismatic leaders are:
1. Clarity of thought and purpose.
2. Attitude to learn and share.

3. Toughness to endure and thrive.
4. Storytelling—an art of leadership.
5. Discipline and hunger drive the leaders.
6. Passion and Purpose.
7. Understand Finances—Investment, Spend and Outcome.
8. Power of Balance—Life vs. Career.
9. Risk Appetite.
10. Importance of having a mentor.
11. When to start your business?

Clarity of Thought

It is easy to say "You should find your why, and then pursue it." But how to find your why, is a big question. Here is a formula that helped me find my why.

Write down what you are good at—EXPERTISE

Write what you would love doing—EXCITEMENT

Write what you will be paid for—EXPERIENCE

Write what the world needs—SWEET SPOT.

You will find your WHY in between these. Besides the above points, there is something called leverage. Your support environment and your surroundings that can help you achieve the why.

Attitude to Learn and Share

Leadership is all about learning and sharing the knowledge that you have. I strongly believe in the concept of "FLOW". If the "flow" does not happen, it leads to pain. Take anything for that matter. Breathe in and stop the flow of air, and the human dies. In plants stop the flow of water from roots to leaves, plants die. It does not have to be related to living things. Same thing happens with knowledge: When it stops flowing, it dies. Hence it is essential to let the knowledge flow by sharing. Un-utilized knowledge becomes a burden.

In fact, any concept that exists today is all because of the flow. We shared teachings, learnings from generations together, so we still see them alive.

Teachers and leaders become a source of flow. When they acquire knowledge and start passing them on, they become eternal. If you have noticed, rich and wealthy people who have shared their knowledge are always remembered. Books, biographies and autobiographies are the ways of sharing your knowledge with the next generation. The kings and scholars did this in the form of manuscripts and inscriptions. Today we know many things about how the world evolved, how people were living back then and how the customs, traditions and cultures came into being.

Toughness to Endure and Thrive

Leaders, as we see, are highly motivated. An important thing to know is they are always alone, fighting a battle that they only understand.

Networking as a Leader in Business

As a leader, the journey is always alone on the top. Especially when it comes to making decisions, drawing a vision statement for your business and company or even sharing lighter moments, you are less likely to find the right people around to share. Hence networking events play a major role in business. Being part of networking organizations not only gives you the picture of what is happening around you, but also helps you to make like-minded friends, discuss your problems as an entrepreneur and sometimes find a mentor for your business.

Storytelling as An Art of Leadership
I have learned this the hard way.

Once I was asked to introduce myself to a very senior woman entrepreneur. It was a great opportunity to showcase my skill-set and my team's strengths and capabilities. We were doing pretty good and this discussion was happening in the mid of the pandemic around July 2020.

I introduced myself as an engineer-turned-entrepreneur. It was just a casual discussion is what I thought. But I never realized that, that one meeting would bring a sea-change in my business. Do you know what happened? I failed miserably in telling my story. I never thought people ever cared why I started and what I was doing. But that day, it dawned upon me, that to make emotional connections, I needed to tell a story which people can relate to, people can understand and connect with.

My mentor taught me how to tell a story and then I started working on it. I started learning how to tell a story that relates to the audience.

Why is Storytelling Important?
As someone rightly said, words could be forgotten, but stories are always remembered. The three C's of a storytelling are Content, Context and Conclusion.

After my failed attempt at telling my story, I started reading many books and articles on storytelling. Paul Smith's—Lead with a story is my favorite book and I would recommend that for all the business leaders. Paul has laid down hundreds of stories, which not only help me on striking a conversation, but impress my audience with effective storytelling.

Here is an example of an effective storytelling, which clearly explains the 3 C's.

Context: Give the context to your story. Story takes place at a time, a place and the state of mind of the person.

Why Context?

Context allows our audience to imagine the scene right in front of them. They can connect, relate and feel for themselves about it.

E.g. "It was July, 2001. I was traveling from Mumbai Airport to the Tata Group Office. It was raining heavily and my car stopped at a signal. Beside my car, I saw a couple on a two-wheeler with two kids completely drenched in the rain waiting for the signal to turn green. It never dawned upon me on that small families cannot afford a car. I realized, all the cars were above their budgetary reach. They were close to Rs. 3-4 Lakhs. There was no car that a middle-class Indian family can afford. That day, I decided to put all my efforts toward manufacturing a car for a middle-class Indian family. A car that every home can afford!" That gave birth to TATA NANO Car. And the man who was traveling in that heavy rain was none other than Mr. Ratan Tata.

Mr. Ratan Tata's story when he launched the TATA NANO spiked a chord with the audience instantly. People quickly realized that TATA Nano was an affordable car for every middle-class person. It needed no advertisements or Marketing. The story itself sold millions of cars thereafter.

That is the power of storytelling.

Content

People hearing your story should take away something when the story is done. They should be going through an emotional path and finally ready to reach a conclusion. The storytelling patterns are different. As explained by Joe Bunting—the author of several books and the owner of "The Write Practice", there are three types of story arcs—Double man in a story arc, Icarus story arc and Oedipus story arc.

If a story does not take the reader through the highs and lows of emotions, it is never a story but just informational content. Thus the arcs of emotions are important in a story.

For e.g., in the story told by Mr. Ratan Tata, the content was very clear. How he was traveling in a car and saw a family drenched in the rain. That was an emotionally low arc.

Then he thought of why middle-class families could not afford a car. That takes the reader to a thinking process too.

The decision to make a car that every middle-class family can afford. That is an emotional high.

Conclusion

This is the key to effective storytelling. Driving your audience to a point, where you want them to be. This is where your audience will know they have a takeaway.

In the case of TATA Nano, the audience took away the point that TATA NANO Car was an affordable car that every household can afford.

Storytelling not only helps people connect with your story, but also helps them relate and make a choice.

Here is an interesting story from a match-making business owner. His business is to help unmarried men and women find their right soulmate. Here is what he says, when he sells his services:

You are in the midst of your career, and your family suggests you get married. You see a girl, fall in love and go on a date. You spend $1000 on the first date, then you go for a couple of more dates after that. Finally, you think she is "THE ONE". One fine day, you propose to her, she agrees and you get married. You spend a million dollars on the wedding. You invite all your friends, family and colleagues to share the moments. Six months down the line, you realize she is not THE ONE. Now you are completely broken, embarrassed to face your family and friends, fight for divorce and finally end up paying alimony.

"With my wedding services, I offer you our services that can save you millions of dollars and emotional trauma. You take a risk-avert route," he says to conclude.

Though this is a funny story, it does drive the audience to a point. Unmarried men and women sign up with his match-making services to avoid the hassles.

Passion and Purpose

Joseph was a young and passionate technology enthusiast. He wanted to excel in whatever he took up. Give him a problem statement and he will ensure that he solves it for you. He never rests until he finds the solution. It is close to seven years that Joseph has been so passionate about his work and solving problems. One day his friend suggested, "Joe, you are so good at solving tech problems, why don't you take up consulting work or start your own business?"

Joe was already thinking about it and when his friend suggested, he thought he should strongly consider that idea. He quickly submitted his resignation and started pursuing his interests in setting up his own business. He hardly knew that business was all about running all the pillars of Marketing, Sales, operations, accounts and HR all at once or simultaneously.

Joe started working on a consulting project before it was his last working day. He was happy that he got an assignment even before he started on his own. This raised his confidence in his decision.

It was his last day at the office. Joe walked into the office, he felt a little nostalgic as he walked in. Since it was his last day at work, his colleagues arranged for a party, they made him feel valued and were sad that he was leaving. Joe was able to connect with their emotions. It was a mix of a roller-coaster of emotions that he was also going through. Sad that he was leaving an organization that he had served for seven long years, excited that he was starting on a new journey, uncertain about what he had in store in the future, happy that he would be working on his own terms and timings, etc. His expressions showed it all. He was confused!

The next day Joe drove himself to a small shared office space that he had rented for his new office. He quietly sat at the corner desk and started writing about what all he had to do for that day. The list was never-ending. He soon realized, he would need the support of a few people and cannot do all of his own. He hired a couple of interns to help him with making a few Sales calls and follow-ups. He continued on the consulting assignment that he started working on while on the notice period.

Six months down the line, he ended up being stuck where he had begun. The project that he consulted for never paid him for the work he had done. Joseph then realized that having just the skills to solve problems is not enough to become successful. He never found the purpose for his business, the discipline to follow-up with the clients was lacking and his hunger to grow was at the least.

After six months he had decided to go back to the corporate world, where everything else is taken care of and he gets to solve the problems that he was passionate about.

Many people often confuse passion and hobby. Passion, they felt, was something that lets you forget your time while you continue to work on it. But that is not always true. Passion lies in doing a work consistently where you can measure your work, measure your quality and improve upon it. There is a growth in passion. Whereas hobby is, you do it when you find the time or when you want to forget time: -)

Purpose
When a passion does not have a purpose, it does not drive for a long time. Like what happened with Joe. He had a passion to solve problems, but did not find a greater purpose that could drive him further.

For many, the purpose is usually beyond earning money. While money is a by-product in any business, there is always a greater purpose behind it.

Discipline

Discipline is one of the key ingredients for the success of any business. The discipline to complete a task, discipline to follow-up, to correct, to open, to close, to start, to end, etc. What is discipline in business? Is it just being on time? Is it just doing what is to be done? Many people ask me this question.

Mr. Vijay is a successful businessman who owns a spare parts shop in a busy street in Mumbai. His customers are basically mechanics, or car dealer stores and car repair shops in and around Mumbai. Though Vijay's customers start working at 10 A.M. and end at 7 P.M., Vijay makes it a point to open his store by 9 A.M. every day. Be it a sunny day, rainy day, whether it is cold winter or hot summer, his store is open at 9 A.M. sharp. He has been following this discipline for the last twenty years. Nothing stops him from serving his customers. Today Vijay is a successful entrepreneur. His employees and his clients love to do business with him.

Vijay was a salesman-turned-entrepreneur. He was passionate about selling things, but never knew he would be a successful entrepreneur one day. One day, Vijay was called into his Manager's office. He was insulted and accused of fraud that he never committed. He was asked to leave immediately, without being explained about the details of the incident of fraud. Vijay was confused, heavy at heart and left his company. Today he says, "It was the most depressing moment of my life. I did not know what to do. I did not tell my family for three days. Finally I realized, I should speak to my parents and wife and tell them." Vijay says "Every adversity is an opportunity." At that moment he realized his strengths, his passion and his commitment to work for the greater good. He took a loan from his family, opened a store, invested in the inventory and started his journey. He respects his family and feels that, had they had not supported him, he would have ended up nowhere.

When asked, what he had learned all these years, he proudly says "Discipline and passion, make you a strong leader."

Discipline is not just about being on time. Discipline is something that you do and stay committed to even if you do not like it. Discipline is like doing your duty and not anticipating the results. This is to be followed in every task you do, every prayer you pray and every person you talk to. Do the due diligence. Do you remember the concept of flow that I explained earlier? Discipline is a flow of events consciously, consistently without any expectation of the results. As Vijay had experienced, everything will fall in place.

* * *

Chapter 11
RISK TOLERANCE FOR ENTREPRENEURS

Ali just passed out of college. Ali was a very enthusiastic guy, who had a lot of ideas. He was popular in his college for all the innovations he did with his crazy ideas. He attended a few interviews, but was rejected. He was disappointed. He did not understand what was going on. He was accompanied by his friends Jay and Tony, who also came to the city in search of a job. Jay was an introvert. He kept things for himself, was hardworking and came from a middle-class background. Tony, on the other hand, was rich, uncompromising and aggressive at times.

Jay and Tony were rejected too, and they were desperate to get a job in a multinational company. Tony was offered a meager salary in a startup, but was not willing to take it, as it would bring down his family reputation. He was only looking for MNCs, CMM Level-3 companies.

Jay on the other hand was rejected for not being outspoken, and unable to communicate well.

One day, Ali, Jay and Tony sat together to discuss their plans for their future. Jay and Tony imagined themselves to be working for MNCs, and Ali was confident of setting up his own business soon. As Ali was telling Jay and Tony about his vision of starting up his business, the innovative ideas he had and the amazing prototypes he had developed, Tony and Jay became more inquisitive. They started asking him all the questions about who inspired him, how was he planning to start, etc.

Two days later, Jay received a call from a multinational company. He was being offered the position of a Junior Software Engineer with a decent package. He soon received an e-mail

"Congratulations, Mr. Jay!

We are happy and delighted to offer you the position of Junior Software Engineer with our company. As a part of continuous learning, you will be attending a six-month training at one of our facilities. Details shall be shared soon by one of our team members. After training the employees shall be assigned to a dedicated workplace.

We welcome you aboard!

Should you have any questions, you can reach out to Mr. Madhu from the HR department.

In response to this e-mail, please share an acceptance note in the next three days.

Thanks & Regards,"

Jay was very happy to see the e-mail and was eagerly waiting to share it with his friends Tony and Ali. As Ali arrived back, he found Jay was unusually happy. Jay shared the news. Ali gave a tight hug and said "Congratulations Jay! I am very happy for you!"

Tony arrived late at night. The next morning, as Tony was getting ready for an interview, Jay shared his happiness with Tony. Tony gave a tight handshake and said, "Congratulations Jay! I knew you would get selected. Your performance was very good at the interview. I had a strong feeling that you will get selected." Jay thanked Tony and wished him good luck for his interview.

A few days later, Jay was sitting in his lounge and thinking about how he had met Tony and Ali. He was still going through those few moments of enthusiasm he had felt when Ali was talking about setting up his own business. His ideas about the business, being your own boss, living at your own terms were somehow fascinating for Jay.

Suddenly his thoughts were interrupted by Ali, who walked to him with a cup of coffee. Ali asked, "Jay, you seem to be lost in your thoughts. Is everything okay?"

Jay replied, "I was just thinking about the discussion we had about you starting your own company."

Ali said, "Yeah, someday I want to set up my own company. I want to innovate and build products for people."

Jay: "Why someday? Why don't you start now? You are intelligent, you are innovative."

Ali: "Actually I registered my company last week. I am trying to add a few people to get things started."

Jay: "That's fantastic. Why didn't you tell us?"

Ali: "I knew you were working hard to get a job at an MNC. I didn't want to distract you from your goal."

Jay: "In fact, after I heard about your dreams, I was starting to think differently. I have not responded to the company's e-mail, accepting the offer. I am still not sure if I should take it or should I join you in your startup?"

Ali felt happy that Jay believed in his vision/dream.

Ali said excitedly "Wow! Jay, I feel so happy that you believe in my dream. But I guess you should take the opinion of your family."

Jay said okay and they left the conversation there.

Five years later when Ali, Jay and Tony met in Mumbai, Jay was working as a Senior Associate Engineer. He was happy with his job and was in a committed relationship. Tony was working with one of his father's friend's sons. He was into gaming. He was very excited about the new animated gaming that they were working on. Ali, on the other hand, was working with a stealth startup as a Junior Engineer with two years' experience.

Jay and Tony were surprised to hear Ali was working for someone else. When they asked, Ali explained how he started, how his dreams got shattered and what he realized after all the mess he had been through.

He said, "Jay, I am really happy to see you today. I think your family's suggestion was quite right for you." He continued, "I started my company with a vision to help people with tech solutions. I realized that just having a dream is not just enough. It needs hard work, dedication, consistency and patience to see what you envision. It needed the right direction, risk-taking appetite and regain the ground if we fall."

Jay and Tony were listening to Ali's words.

Ali continued to explain where he went wrong. He said "I thought building a product itself is enough. I was fascinated by many companies that started small. But I guess I was wrong. I never considered Marketing and Sales and customer service at all."

Jay curiously asked, "What about the pre-seed funding you raised?"

Ali replied, "Yeah, we received a pre-seed funding. But I guess I was with the wrong people who took the wrong decisions. I feel guilty that I spent investors' money without justifying it. So I came out of it and joined another organization. I am learning a lot currently. I am sure, I will start up on my own again after a few years."

Jay and Tony were happy that Ali still had the fire to restart his company. The dream he had in him did not die.

After hearing this story, I remembered the words one of my elderly friends once said to me: "Entrepreneurial journey is all about the risk appetite of an individual." The risk he mentions is not only financial but the risking of social status, your career, your free time, your income, etc. The journey of an entrepreneur is about the ability to take risks and thrive under pressure.

Many young people consider innovativeness, proactiveness, big dreams and hope as the signs of entrepreneurship. They take the plunge and eventually fail.

However, once in the path of entrepreneurship and handling everything by themselves, they realize entrepreneurship is more than just the list of things mentioned above. Some throw the towel too early and some continue to correct themselves and pursue further like Ali.

> *Mistakes: Having too small margins.*
>
> *Misconception: Anyone can become an entrepreneur*
>
> *Truth: Entrepreneurs strive long, they stay in the game for a long time, they believe in their dreams, they are passionate and thrive in the toughest circumstances.*

* * *

Chapter 12
IDENTIFYING YOUR STRENGTHS

Finding our purpose is the biggest mystery we need to solve. Once you know your purpose, you focus your energies on it and ensure your purpose is achieved. Unfortunately, many people do not live long enough to discover their purpose. But as I say, every life has a meaning, a purpose. We forget about it, as we get distracted by many enticing things that come our way.

We all are born with unique strengths. We come across unique situations and emotional connections as we grow up. We all know, though born in the same family, our siblings are much different from ourselves. Even twins, though born at the same time, may see their own world differently. Because, we have different circumstances, emotions, feelings, beliefs and attitudes.

Here is a story of twins who perceived their life differently though born together. Geet and Sagar were twins, born in Bhopal, the capital city of Madhya Pradesh, India. They grew up in a nuclear family. Geet grew up to become a responsible father, taking care of his family. Sagar, on the other hand, had trouble keeping up his day-job and was in bad company with people. He had a troubled relationship with his wife and children. Was mostly seen drunk and depressed. You may ask, why was there so much difference in their attitudes and behaviors?

Each of them perceived their worlds differently.

While Geet learned how not to be like their father, Sagar likened himself to be like his father.

They both grew up in a troubled home. Constant fights, hard conversations are what they heard as they grew up. And both Geet and Sagar perceived things differently.

Geet found that his purpose in life was to take care of his family. He ensured that his wife and kids were happy with him. He strived to always give all the support his family needed from him.

Sagar, on the other hand, wanted to be like his father. Ferocious, angry and getting things done anyway.

Though born in the same family, we might have different purposes. Here are a few things to ponder upon, when finding your purpose:

- What are my strengths?
- What were those things that kept me motivated when I was young?
- What were the unique circumstances that brought out my strengths?
- What are the problems I see in the world, which keep me awake in the night?
- Can I solve those problems with my skills, attitude and strengths that I have acquired over the years?

As I always say, we all are born with huge potential and huge energy in ourselves. As said in many books, we are born for the greater purpose, a purpose that we have to identify ourselves. The circumstances, situations and the environment around teach us a lot. Being vary of all those things and moving forward with a vision in mind make us see the bigger picture. People fail to see the bigger picture, as they are constantly interrupted by smaller situations and circumstances. Some see these as a challenge and either quit or move forward.

When I found my Why, I was surprised. I knew I had it all through my mind, but that did not take the first seat initially. Empowering women, creating as much employment as possible has now become my mission. My objective is to empower them financially, psychologically and emotionally.

I got inspired by my mother, who always has a passion to do something. She does not sit idle and always has a creative side of her that entices her. In her younger days, it was no different. She wanted to work as a teacher, but bringing up three children took the front seat in her life. My father was working away for most of his life. So my mother had to take care of us.

She had the fire in her to do something and build her own career. But she prioritized us, than her desires. She started taking tuitions for school children. We had many parents and students visiting our home to talk to my mother. I understood that her passion drives her. She was a successful teacher who balanced life, career and her dreams. There are many women, who are passionate, but priorities change after their marriage and kids. My mission is to give opportunities for people to grow and excel in what they love to do. Empower all those women by giving them opportunities to balance life, career and dreams.

And as I told you, it was not an 'Aha-moment' for me. It slowly evolved. I was subconsciously tuned to see this happen. I tried to help a few women. It was not impossible. I saw them happy, balanced and able to drive their passion and dreams. The happiness in them made me realize my purpose. My dream, my goal!

So, if you want to find your 'Why?' keep looking around. Take time to think, realize and achieve your goals and dreams.

This is possibly the case with everyone else. As Michelle Obama rightly said in her memoir—Becoming: "Becoming is not about arriving somewhere or achieving a certain aim. I see it instead as forward motion, a means of evolving, a way to reach continuously toward a better self. The journey doesn't end." The journey to life is never-ending. It is constantly evolving.

> *"For me, becoming isn't about arriving somewhere or achieving a certain aim. I see it instead as forward motion, a means of evolving, a way to reach continuously toward a better self. The journey doesn't end."*
>
> *– Michelle Obama*

* * *

Chapter 13
MINDSET VS. SKILL-SET

Rehan and Aaron were good friends. They knew each other from their college days. While Rehan was a happy-go-lucky guy, Aaron was hardworking. Rehan was an immigrant who went to the US with big dreams for himself and his parents. He wanted to work with the best people in the world. He had a knack for making conversations fun when people were around him.

Aaron was a Native American, who had been inspired by the likes of Elon Musk and Jeff Bezos. He strongly believed in hard work and was always looking at the brighter side of his life. Both his parents were government servants. He had always heard from them about the savings, 401K, etc. Aaron always aspired to be an entrepreneur who does not have to depend on 401K and savings and will plan his own investments to yield good financial returns.

Rehan and Aaron started working in an electronic chip manufacturing company. Both worked hard in their initial days to impress their bosses and cement their positions. Rehan focused more on learning the work and doing things that his boss wanted him to do. Aaron, on the other hand, focused on learning new skills along with understanding how the company works. He would stay late in the evenings talking to colleagues in other departments to know whom they worked for and what their departments were focused on. Aaron was focused on getting a bigger picture.

A few years later Aaron and Rehan met at the cafeteria. They sat down to discuss how they have been doing. Rehan told Aaron about his plans for moving up the ladder. He wanted to apply for a promotion. Aaron announced that he had already resigned and would be starting up his new company soon. Rehan was excited and congratulated Aaron.

Aaron took a small office space in the suburbs of the city. He started working with his friend Mike, whom he met at his previous company and shared the same energy as Aaron. Both Aaron and Mike were excited for the first few months. They were proud to announce that they started their own electronic company. Their idea was to help other electronic companies with procurement hassles. Aaron and Mike had a solution in mind that can help the electronic companies procure raw material and spares at a much better price. They ground in the best quality and price to the table.

While Aaron was prepared that it would take time to stabilize their business, Mike was not sharing a similar thought-process. Nine months down the line, Mike offered to quit as he felt that things were not going in the way he expected. Aaron's persuasions did not bring any change in Mike's decision. Aaron continued to work on his business, and found other like-minded people to join his team. Five months after Mike left, Aaron got a big project. He soon became busy with the negotiations, quotations, vendor onboarding, etc. The clients were so impressed with Aaron's and his team's work that they signed a contract with his company. Aaron's company now is a vendor partner for that chip-making company. Soon his old company also approached him to take up the procurement vendorship. Today after five years, Aaron has a team of more than a hundred people who work with him. Has more than fifteen clients and runs a multimillion-dollar company.

Like Aaron, when starting up your own business, you may find the journey exciting in the beginning. Many people know their skill-set and strengths. They start up with a lot of enthusiasm. The enthusiasm stays there for the first few months. Then they slowly settle in to understand the reality. Sometimes products do not sell, people do not sign up for the subscriptions. They start feeling uncomfortable and decide to quit.

To be successful you need to have these two basic qualities in you -patience and perseverance. Are these qualities just enough? I say "No". These are just two pieces of the larger puzzle. While you wait with perseverance and patience, you still have to be hardworking, stay hungry, have financial backup to persevere and keep learning.

We all know that we have specific skillsets that we have built up over time. We work hard, we pick up the skills of getting things done or doing things in a particular way. But those skillsets make only 20% of what you actually need for your business. 80% of your business success depends on your mindset. This includes perseverance, patience, focus, vision, learning, applying your learnings, etc. Unfortunately, many of these things are not taught anywhere in the world. You have to jump into a business to learn them. As I always say—Hate it or love it, life is the best teacher anyone can have. You will see its teachings when you are ready to learn.

> "Hate it or Love it, Life is the best teacher anyone can have. You will see its teachings, only when you are ready to learn."
>
> – Prashanthi Kolluru

Many people ask me why I chose Marketing to achieve my vision of empowering women. I feel very happy when someone asks this question. Women do many things differently than men. Especially being a mother teaches a lot. When a child is not able to understand a message, a mother tries to make the child understand the message in several different ways. She uses all her creative storytelling, incident narration, etc. to help the child understand the essence. I feel Marketing is no different.

We understand the product, identify the target audience. When we run a Marketing campaign we try different campaigns to make sure the message is reached to the audience. The message could be an awareness campaign, a promotional event or a new product launch. This ultimately ensures that your audience is able to understand the message.

Business is all about growing yourself and discovering yourself. Your strengths, your weaknesses, your flaws, your positives, etc. Being in business teaches you perseverance, patience, discipline, hard work, commitment to yourself. Every day, you have new things to learn, apply, evolve and grow. It made me strong; it made me a different person altogether. And this is the road less taken. But when taken, you have to commit yourself to give it your best shot. Commit to yourself that nothing will bring you down.

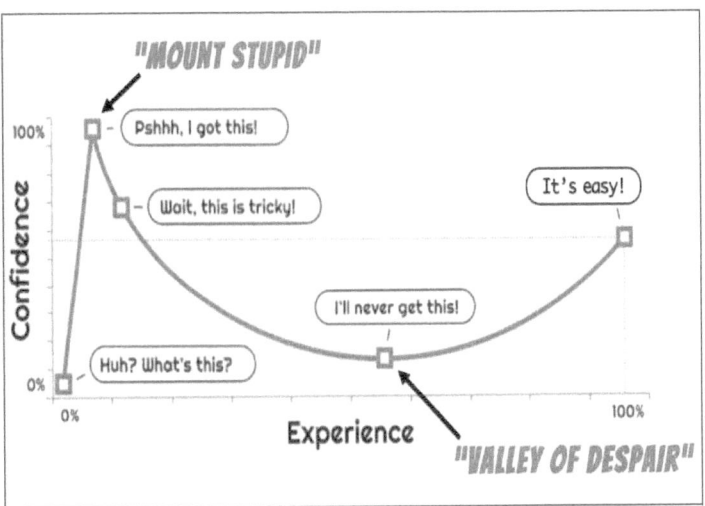

Kruger Effect graph explains a few interesting facts about cognitive bias. It explains how people at a low ability of a task overestimate their ability. It is no different in real life.

If you see people laughing at your mistakes and failures, just know that they overestimating their ability, who never took the path less- traveled. I have come across many people who mocked me, who made fun of me… But that just kept making me stronger. Because, all I could do is to change myself, and I chose to become stronger every day. The strength in me made me look up high, leaving all those people behind and fly like a rocket, that can never be reached. I realized my strengths, my vision and my commitment to my vision. It keeps making me strong every day.

* * *

Chapter 14
POWER OF LEVERAGE

Sudha and Sarina are women who aspire to become business owners. They completed their MBAs and worked for a couple of startups before starting on their own. Sudha is married to Anurag and is blessed with an adorable son—Ranit. Anurag aspires to be a business owner himself. However, he feels Sudha can take up the business part, while he continues to support her.

Sarina is married to Stanley. They are blessed with a beautiful daughter Anika and an adorable son Anirudh. Stanley works as a Software Engineer and often travels to the US on business. Stanley is more concerned about his family and prefers Sarina to stay at home and take care of the kids. Though Sarina conveyed to Stanley about her aspirations to start her own business, Stanley kept postponing, saying "Let's do it once the kids grow up." Sarina had been trying to keep her fire alive for many years, waiting for Stanley to give his approval. But that never comes up. And by the time their kids grew up, Sarina lost that fire and does not aspire anymore.

Sudha, on the other hand, tries different businesses. She fails, she learns. Anurag keeps educating her about the mistakes done and how they can overcome them. Anurag supports Sudha not only in business but also in the household chores. He has hired a full-time maid who can take care of the mundane works, while Sudha can focus on her business part.

A few years into the business, constantly failing and learning, Sudha realizes her strength lies in Marketing. She continues to pursue her interest in Marketing, acquires new clients and delivers to client expectations. Today she has a team of 53+ people who help various clients with their Marketing activities.

Sudha credits her success to her husband and son and her family who had constantly motivated her. She understands that Anurag's support has been tremendous and that without his support, she would not have been successful.

Did you notice the power of leverage that Sudha had?

Sudha had a supportive family; she had the fire inside her to start a new business. She had the necessary skill-set to achieve her dreams. And every time she failed, Anurag was there to hold her back.

> *"If you have a leverage in life, it becomes your responsibility to become successful."*
>
> *– Prashanthi Kolluru*

Leverage is another most important factor when you are running a business. Not many business owners are lucky to have a leverage in their life. And if you have it, then it becomes your responsibility to become successful in what you are doing.

I have seen many business owners and aspiring business people, who either took off and landed in a mess or never took off. When analyzed on why they ended up in a mess, we understand that they did not have enough leverage to play around and experiment enough.

As quoted by Malcolm Galdwell in his book Outliers, leverage plays a very important role in anyone's life. If you look at the life of Bill Gates from a leverage perspective, you will understand it in detail

What we all know is Bill Gates became the richest man in the world. But how did he do it? What were the leverages he got? How did he use his leverage and his passion to pursue a dream of becoming an entrepreneur? Here is a small account.

Bill Gates was born into an educated family that encouraged competitiveness. His father was a lawyer and his mother was a school teacher. Bill Gates was a voracious reader from childhood. But at the age of eleven or twelve, his parents became concerned about his behavior. He was bored and showed signs of withdrawal. They were worried he might become a loner. Hence, they enrolled him at a Lakeside School where most of the rich kids in Seattle, WA would go. Many rich parents could afford it. It was a boarding school with a huge library. A few months after Gates joined, there was a proposal to open a computer lab in the school.

The Mother's club of the school contributed to the schools' donations to open a computer lab. A Seattle computer company offered computer time for students. The school agreed to open a terminal for its students' benefit. In those days, computers were the size of a room. It was when Gates was thirteen years old, that he wrote his first computer program. Those days the programs were written on punch cards. These cards were to be inserted into the computer to run it. One had to wait for hours in queue to check his program. And if the program failed, the person would take at least one week to correct the program, before he could re-test it again. Gates was spending most of his free time at the terminal. A few years later the computer lab was closed, due to some issues. Gates, however, found an opportunity to work as an intern at a nearby company, which was looking to develop their payroll program for their employees. While in the weekdays, Gates would do his school work and most of the weekends, he would be spending time at the company developing their payroll software. By then the computers had evolved and were no more the size of a room.

It was at the Lakeside School, where Gates met his longtime partner Paul Allen. Paul Allen was senior to Bill Gates and shared similar interests as him. It was said that Gates, Allen and a few others had their terminal privileges revoked as they took advantage of a computer glitch to obtain more free computer time.

After Gates completed high school, he applied for Harvard to enroll in Law program. He dropped off two years later to pursue his entrepreneurial dreams. In 1975 Gates along with Paul Allen founded Micro-Soft, later renamed Microsoft.

What Were the Leverages That Gates Had?

His parents were rich, who could afford to buy books for him to become inquisitive at an early age. The family had a competitive outlook and the kids were rewarded for winning and punished for losing. Hence the kids always tried to excel in whatever they did. Parents could afford to send Bill Gates to the richest school in Seattle, which afforded a computer terminal in those days. Gates' interest in computers was noticed by the

Seattle computer company, who later gave Gates and Allen an opportunity to work on their Payroll Software. Finally by the time Gates started his own company in 1975, he had written more than 10,000 lines of code and was a pro at software.

Here are a few mistakes entrepreneurs do, taking Bill Gates as an example. They consider him as a role model for all different reasons.

I have come across a few startup entrepreneurs who fancied calling themselves college drop-outs and likening themselves to Bill Gates, starting their own company at a young age, etc. When asked what they would like to become, their usual answer was—to found a company like Microsoft and Apple. Though they copy every aspect of what Bill Gates and Steve Jobs had done earlier in life, they overlook the most important point—Leverage.

Being cognizant of the concept of leverage can give any aspiring entrepreneurs an edge to become successful.

※ ※ ※

Chapter 15
IMPORTANCE OF A MENTOR

Many business owners tend to see themselves as know-all, tell-all. They focus more on running a business mostly unguided. They try to swim in the ocean without a trainer. And trust me, many of them fail. Some realize that they need someone to guide and assist them. So they start in search of a mentor.

Mentors are typically the teachers who guide you through the business. They become your best critics and stand with you tall when you need them. I am lucky to find a few mentors in my life, who are closely associated with me. They guide me through every step and give me direction.

Many great entrepreneurs had got mentors or coaches themselves. Here is a short story of Bill (William) Campbell, who coached Billionaires like Zuckerberg, Larry Page and Steve Jobs and Tim Cook, Eric Schmidt, Sundar Pichai, Sheryl Sandberg, etc.

According to a biography "Trillion Dollar Coach", Bill Campbell was a football coach at Columbia University. As a coach in a football game, he understood the power of a team and how a team can be mentored and steered in, to achieve the team's objectives. And Bill saw corporates were no different. It is always teamwork, love, trust and people that make enterprises achieve their goals.

Why Does a Business Owner Need a Mentor?

A mentor is a person, who has-been-there, done that. His focus is more to bring the best in you.

Early in life, when growing up, we learn a lot from our teachers, parents, peers, friends, etc. However, when an entrepreneur takes up his journey, unfortunately, many forget where they had come from. As said earlier, they jump into the ocean and then complain about drowning.

We all need mentors in our business. A person who can guide us in the right direction, make us focus on the goals and keep us motivated to achieve those goals. Here are a few benefits of having a mentor:

1. They bring their experience to the table, which is not taught in the self-help books that we read.
2. Eighty percent of business owners owe their success to mentors. The success factor with a mentor is higher. You are more likely to succeed if you have a mentor in your business.
3. Mentors can open up a whole new network of opportunities for your business. Especially when it comes to you seeking investments, a mentor can introduce you to tap the investors in his network, who are more likely to invest, than in any other random startup.
4. Mentors help you build your EQ. Emotional Intelligence is a crucial factor in determining the success or failure of a business. As we all know, we do not make logical decisions. Our decisions are mostly emotional; we apply logic to our decisions and justify them. Many businesses fail due to emotional decision-making. Having a mentor

in your business not only helps you make smart decisions but also leads you toward the success path.

5. Encouragement: Many business owners face depression when they are unable to achieve their business goals. But having an experienced mentor around can prevent the entrepreneur from slipping into depression. The mentor keeps the fire alive in the entrepreneur and makes him focus in the right direction.

Chapter 16

WHY PERFECTIONISTS MAY FIND IT DIFFICULT TO THRIVE IN BUSINESS?

Being a perfectionist is what we all have been taught when we were young. Perfection was rewarded and imperfections were punished. Hence these get hardcoded in our subconscious minds so well that we carry it through our adulthood and sometimes impose it on our children too. But one thing that we always forget to notice or understand is there is nothing called 'perfect' in real life. Every person is unique, every tree is unique and every organism on this earth is unique. And if everything and everyone is perfect, there is nothing anyone can think about.

Unfortunately, many of us carry this "Perfectionism" into business as well. Many business owners strive for perfection. They want to do all things right from day-one. They find the perfect name, perfect brand logo; they find everything perfect and get it done. But by the time, they get a perfect of everything, they lose sight of the important parameters like market relevancy, product/service opportunity and most importantly the time.

If you are a perfectionist and aspire to become an entrepreneur, you should start loosening up a little. Nothing is perfect, it is all a myth and your perception. Accept and get over with it.

Perfectionists tend to believe in "If you want to do it right, then do it yourself." And if a perfectionist becomes an entrepreneur, he would not trust anyone. He/she would have a difficult time in accepting anyone else's work. Sometimes, perfectionists are seen to be suffering from emotional outbursts, depression, stress and anxiety. And these are not good signs to become entrepreneurs.

Steve Jobs was a perfectionist, who had emotional outbursts at times. He would ask his employees to get his approval on every single detail. He had emotional outbursts and would often fire people without giving a second thought. However, as soon as he realized that this style of management would not allow Apple Inc to grow, he started working on his personal development. If he had not accepted his weakness toward perfectionism, Apple would not have been where it is today.

What is Success in Life or Business?

Many entrepreneurs believe that setting up a goal and achieving that goal is a success in business. The reason behind this is, we are tuned like that from childhood and school days. We are taught about success and failure differently in schools. A student who secures a target score is tagged as successful and moved to the next grade, and the student who does not reach is tagged a failure, and not promoted. Thus we tend to attribute success to achieving a target or a goal. That is a misconception that every entrepreneur goes through.

The mistake we do is, we attribute the same measure in life and business. We set up a financial target for a year, achieve it and feel successful. What happens next, we reel in the success for a little longer and forget to set the goal for the next year. Then we fail.

Success is all about being consistent. You should be able to achieve your targets and goals consistently and stay in the race. That is success!

A business is considered successful when it achieves its financial and business goals consistently year on year. As rightly said, "Success is a Journey, Not a Destination."

> *If you don't know where you are going, then how will you know when you get there?*
>
> *– Dr. Stephen Covey*

* * *

FINAL WORDS

Starting up with your own business is a dream for many. This is a big dream that starts with a small step. Many enthusiasts are worried to take the first few steps. They are worried or do not know where to start.

After having read this far, I am sure you will be ready to start on your own and take that first crucial step. Remember the following key points:

1. Success always happens with the very first steps. Get started, persevere to continue and have the patience to see the results.
2. Be flexible to change strategies. If something is not working, try to make adjustments.
3. Find your "Why?"
4. Keep your focus on achieving your "Why?"
5. Fail Early, Learn Early and just keep going.

SHORT POEM DEDICATED TO ENTREPRENEURS

Winds threaten,
With Dark clouds overcast
Shaking my feet off the ground
Leaving me a choice to succumb or grow.

My mind says to succumb
My heart says to grow
Confused between both,
I ponder with my thoughts to succumb or grow!

A light begins to show up
A hope begins to shine
Just like the sun
In a bright daylight.

Here I am,
Standing tall and strong
Choosing not to succumb,
But to grow and grow!

ABOUT THE AUTHOR

I was a happy-go-lucky girl working with an MNC, enjoying my work and life. I was passionate about my work, looking forward to many opportunities my life was ready to unfold.

All my dreams got stuck after I got married and relocated with my husband. We relocated to the US for a brief period. I was working for an MNC.

It was so painful to leave my eighteen-month-old son at a Daycare and go to work. I was simultaneously searching for an opportunity to work from home. I asked my friends if they could refer me, I searched online for many opportunities. But all I found was fake schemes and form-filling kind of jobs which appeared like a scam. I felt defeated and disappointed.

As I discussed my situation with a few of my friends, I came to realize that many women have no choice but to take a career break post-delivery or go through the same painful circumstances that I went through. It kept questioning me, how can I create opportunities for women, so they can manage their career, and life?

Can I help women to continue to work from home and stay in their career path without taking a career break? If yes, then how can I do it?

In 2014, I started my own business. And my first collaboration was with my childhood friend, mother of two handsome boys with a happy family. We worked remotely, trying to make things happen. I increased my team strength to include more and more women, working in the comfort of their home and staying in their career path.

I dedicate this book to all those beautiful and strong women, who are willing to make a difference in this world.

This book is an attempt to help women look at their own strengths and start working toward their purpose.

While exploring many areas in life, being a home-maker, an employee and an employer myself, I have seen myself in different circumstances. Through this book, I provoke my audience to shake up, know their potential and achieve their purpose in life. There is nothing stopping them, except their thoughts.

This book revolves around how to start your own business. Upon reading this book, you will feel empowered to start on your own and take that first leap into your business. It is not difficult, not easy and not impossible. It will teach you the mistakes people make, so you can learn and not repeat them when you start your business.

This is a short attempt to empower and encourage more women to come into business and stand on their own. Business is not about making money; it is all about, empowering, evolving and discovering yourself.

www.ingramcontent.com/pod-product-compliance
Lightning Source LLC
Chambersburg PA
CBHW021547200526
45163CB00016B/2756